WHAT'S IN A NAME?

Perspectives from Nonbiological and
Nongestational Queer Mothers

Edited by Sherri Martin-Baron,
Raechel Johns, and Emily Regan Wills

T0294419

DEMETER

What's in a name
Perspectives from Nonbiological and Nongestational Queer Mothers
Edited by Sherri Martin-Baron, Raechel Johns, and Emily Regan Wills
Copyright © 2020 Demeter Press

Demeter Press
2546 10th Line
Bradford, Ontario
Canada, L3Z 3L3
Tel: 289-383-0134
Email: info@demeterpress.org
Website: www.demeterpress.org

Demeter Press logo based on the sculpture "Demeter" by Maria-Luise Bodirsky www.keramik-atelier.bodirsky.de

Printed and Bound in Canada

Cover design and typesetting: Michelle Pirovich

Library and Archives Canada Cataloguing in Publication
Title: What's in a name?: Perspectives from nonbiological and nongestational queer mothers / edited by Sherri Martin-Baron, Raechel Johns, and Emily Regan Wills.
Names: Martin-Baron, Sherri, 1977- editor. | Johns, Raechel, 1976- editor. | Wills, Emily Regan, 1981- editor.
Description: Includes bibliographical references.
Identifiers: Canadiana 20200257528 | ISBN 9781772582376 (softcover)
Subjects: LCSH: Nonbiological mothers. | LCSH: Nonbiological mothers —Psychology. | LCSH: Sexual minority parents. | LCSH: Sexual minority parents—Psychology. | LCSH: Parenthood. | LCSH: Parenthood— Psychological aspects. | LCSH: Motherhood. | LCSH: Motherhood— Psychological aspects.
Classification: LCC HQ73.6 .W43 2020 | DDC 306.874/30866—dc23

Acknowledgments

The editors, Sherri, Raechel, and Emily, would like to acknowledge the support of Demeter Press and in particular Dr. Andrea O'Reilly and Jesse O'Reilly-Conlin. Without Demeter Press, this book would not be here. Demeter Press supports publications around parenting, and particularly motherhood. When the editors were first discussing the book, Demeter Press was our first preference for a publisher, and we were thrilled when they liked the idea.

We would also like to acknowledge all of the contributors. Your stories have made us laugh, cry, and ponder, and we thank you for all of your thoughtful contributions. We also acknowledge you, the reader! We hope you love the stories that have been shared with you.

Sherri would like to acknowledge with gratitude her coeditors, Raechel and Emily, for their confidence in this project and support in bringing it to fruition. It has been a labour of love. She also thanks them for their encouragement to write her own chapter. Sherri would also like to thank two friends, Dr. Emily Perkins and Michelle Loheac, who read early drafts and gave marvelous suggestions for editing her own chapter. She feels grateful to live and work in a community of writers and readers. Lastly, Sherri wishes to thank her family, friends, and colleagues for their love and support, especially her close childhood friends Stacey and Lily, her brother and his family, her parents and parents-in-law, her wife Michelle, who has been her rock, and their three wonderful children.

This project is an interesting blend of family and work, more so than many other projects. As such, when reflecting on acknowledgments, Raechel would like to thank everyone who has supported her in all of her varied roles—professor, parent, wife, daughter, sister, friend, colleague, writer, leader, and so on. Raechel would like to acknowledge the support of her university, the University of Canberra, for supporting her to work on this book. Raechel is grateful for the support of all her family. To her partner and children – this book would not be possible without you! She would also like to thank her broader family (parents, sisters, in-laws, etc.) for all the support provided to her, her partner, and children since they embarked on this crazy parenting journey!

Raechel would also like to acknowledge Sherri for the idea to undertake this project. Sherri shared the idea in a Facebook group. From there, Raechel and Emily joined Sherri to plan the project. This project came to fruition because Sherri had the courage to reach out and suggest she wanted to make this book.

Emily would like to acknowledge the support received from a publication grant from the Faculty of Social Sciences at the University of Ottawa to underwrite the costs of producing this book. In addition, she would like to thank everyone who supports her in balancing parenting and writing. At work, that means her colleagues Nadia Abu-Zahra and Diana El Richani for creating a team where care work is as important as paid work, her department, which never minds having small people wandering the hallways, and her students who accept and even seem to enjoy the chaos. At home, that means her nonbio sister Isabel, her mom Rose, and, most of all, her wife Kate, who has had the harder job for about twelve years now and is really due her own sabbatical.

Contents

Any Other Name: Why We Edited This Book

Sherri Martin-Baron, Raechel Johns,
and Emily Regan Wills

Queer parenthood: It's multifaceted. It's complex. And it is constantly changing, as laws and culture shift around us. What are our experiences as modern queer parents? The voices we often hear are from the biological or gestational parent; however, just as important are the voices of the "other" parent, who often hold a complicated relationship to whatever title they use. This book is a collection of personal essays by queer women and nonbinary people who are nonbiological and nongestational mothers/parents. Our essays explore our experiences parenting across our different social and familial locations. We have all taken different routes to parenting, live in different countries, and understand our relationships to parenting through our own personal lenses. What we all share is a commitment to parenting beyond the limits of biology and of building families that are drawn together and maintained by the love and labour of parenting.

Sherri

When I tell people that my eldest child, now five, still prefers her other mother, I usually get reassurance that parental preferences change. But I worry that's never going to happen. You see, I am the nonbiological and nongestational mother. I didn't grow my child in my body. She doesn't have my DNA, and I couldn't stay at home for the first few months of her life, as my wife was able to through maternity leave at her job. Does my child love me and enjoy spending time with me? Yes. But would she prefer her other mother? Always. I am hopeful that as she gets older, this will even out a little. But that doesn't change the complicated feelings I have about this issue. Very few of my friends in my daily life are nonbiological or nongestational mothers like me. I can share my anxieties and experiences with others, but I'm not sure that they quite understand the nuances.

When my wife was pregnant with our firstborn, I tried to read up on what to expect as a new parent. I found only one book that was meant for people like me, and I honestly found it quite depressing. I appreciated and wanted stories that were complex, yes, but also positive.

So instead, I searched online for queer new parent forums and found one that resonated with me. One night after an exchange on this forum about the lack of resources for queer nonbiological and nongestational mothers, I realized with absolute clarity that if the resources we need aren't out there for us, we need to create them. We will make our own book! I wanted to put our voices out there, for ourselves to build that support, and for others to begin to understand our experiences.

I reached out to this online community of queer mothers from around the world and put my idea out there. The response was overwhelmingly positive, so I decided to move forwards and found support and partnership along the way.

What I have enjoyed most about this process, besides working with two extraordinary coeditors, is communicating with our contributors. Most of our email exchanges have been very businesslike, polite, and brief. But others have been lengthier conversations, sometimes revealing tiny parts of ourselves or showing understanding or sympathy about our personal experiences. I had no idea that this would be part of putting together this book collection. But it makes sense: My desire to have this community see itself in what they read means that I get to see and reveal myself as well.

Writing my own piece was not something I had originally intended to do. Instead, I was intensely focused on the desire to build a community resource and give voice to positive, real stories. It was through this community that I was encouraged to write, even though I had never considered myself a writer. It has been truly an honour to help put these voices together and I am proud to be among them.

Raechel

Some young kids spend their days playing house-type games. They talk about their lives when they have children in the future. They dream about their sons and daughters. Sometimes, they even plan their future careers around parenting. And when they start dating, talking about having a family is a natural transition for them. This was not the case for me. I wasn't going to have children, and now I do—happily, I should add. My chapter shares my story, so I won't repeat it, but the point is that once I seriously considered having children, I wanted, perhaps needed, to read about parenting to get a sense of it all. Because I hadn't imagined it forever, I needed a crash course on parenting. In particular, I wanted to read about same-sex couples raising kids and conception stories. I wanted to read about identity as a parent. I read everything I could get my hands on, and I loved those stories, but I knew there was space for more. And that's where my role in this book came in.

Sherri reached out in a Facebook community; she wanted to read more queer positive stories and asked whether anyone was interested in discussing creating a book. I contacted her immediately. I am a keen writer, and academic, and knew that our stories could help people plan their families or navigate becoming a nonbiological or nongestational parent.

I'm in so many social media communities, and in these groups, you often see posts at points of crisis. I often read stories from people worried about attachment and bonding. Some people talk about their discomfort when someone mentions that the baby looks like them or looks like their partner. I have read stories about people who wanted to carry a child but couldn't, and in passing the baton to their partner, they felt incredibly envious rather than excited as their partner's belly grew. It's wonderful participating in these discussions and providing support on social media, but they don't offer a full story or resolution, in the way the chapters in this book do. Many times people also reach out for support during a difficult time in their lives but don't share the positives. The chapters in this book vary—some cover a relatively short period of time (for example, conception), whereas others cover a longer time, such as an entire decade of parenting—but each chapter provides a story of a journey towards nonbiological and nongestational parenting that is beautiful and shows wonderful attachments created out of love. The positives are there, with some day-to-day challenges, too.

Whether you read for entertainment, to learn, or because, like me, you want to understand how other families have navigated it all, I'm sure you'll love the stories in this book. Some will make you laugh, some might make you cry, and some will, no doubt, have you nodding along in familiarity. I'm so thrilled that these stories are now out in the world. They contain perspectives from a variety of countries, but many of the feelings are shared among the writers and their families.

I'm so pleased I had an opportunity to contribute in a small way towards getting them to you, the reader. When I embarked on my own parenting journey and tracked down stories to help my understanding, I never imagined one day I would be involved in a project like this, and I'm so proud that I have been. I wish you well in your parenting journey, however it happens.

Emily

I am an odd creature: I find tremendous comfort in complicated social theory. When my wife and I were preparing to get her pregnant, I was reading *The Ultimate Lesbian Guide to Conception and Pregnancy* along with her, but also Honneth's *The Struggle for Recognition* and Bartkey's *Femininity and Domination*, along with a dozen other abstruse books of continental political theory because that was my job right then as a graduate student about to start my dissertation. I inseminated my wife in our bedroom between rounds of working on my comprehensive exam; my thesis proposal defense was scheduled as early in the term as possible so I'd be sure she wasn't going into labour as I was arguing about the relationship between power, discourse, and struggle.

Theory matters to me because it helps me understand my world; it helps me make sense of my feelings and make sense of how things work. bell hooks writes the following in "Theory as Liberatory Practice": "I came to theory desperate, wanting to comprehend--to grasp what was happening around and within me. Most importantly, I wanted to make the hurt go away. I saw in theory then a location for healing." This healing function of theory has always been central for me in how I experience it and in why I keep turning to it.

In this book, I see us beginning to write a theory of mothering/parenting beyond biology. My experience as a mother has been one of struggle against my own limits and constraints, against heteronormative assumptions and biases in law and social relations, against the capitalist devaluing of care labour within the household, and against the wear and strain that all of this work can put on our love and our lives. It has also been an experience of building joy and connection, of casting my net wide and finding the other ends held by people who love me, and of watching my children grow into my wife's freckles and my bad attitude.

We, the writers in this book, wrestle with what it means to not have the bodily experience of growing a child or what it means to not share a genetic relationship with our children. We turn over what it means to have our dreams of pregnancy disrupted and what it means that we never dreamed of it at all but still found ourselves with babies in our arms. We look at the social relations that demand we account for ourselves over and over again, and we both resent it and appreciate the chance it gives us to articulate ourselves to ourselves. We look at our children and imagine how we can narrate ourselves to them.

As a community of queer mothers/parents thinking about our parenting beyond biology, we are doing some of this necessary work of sketching out a first path through this theoretical terrain. As you read this book, I hope that you find that our theory feeds yours and can do some of the work of helping us all heal.

Conclusion

As editors, we went back and forth a great deal about how to organize this collection of essays. After all, there is so much that connects these stories, and each author talks about different issues that have an impact on their parenting experience. As we received and read each chapter, we realized that there were a number of themes that echo each other, with each author describing their own path to and experience of being a parent. We originally tried to group the chapters by theme, but there was so much overlap that we found it was impossible. However, we think you may find many of these themes throughout the chapters, and we hope that they help you reflect on your experience as well.

One of the major themes is the particular struggles that come with being a parent, especially a nonbiological or nongestational one, such as Sherri's story about her relationship with her daughter and her agony over sometimes feeling unwanted by her. Other struggles are specific to how the writers' identities affect their parenthood, such as Jax's reflections on their experience as a disabled parent as well as a disability activist in the context of assisted reproductive technology, which can reproduce many ableist and heteronormative assumptions, or Allie's experience of navigating parenthood as a masculine-of-centre mom when motherhood is so closely associated with femininity. At other times in the book, moments of crisis help resolve ongoing debates—such as, the clarity Ryann experiences when their son is born premature and how their ambivalence about the gendered concept of motherhood is eclipsed by their love for their baby. All of the parents face struggles in the work of parenting. For these authors, these struggles are deeply connected to being a nonbiological and a nongestational mother.

These mothers are not always immediately recognized as parents by the law or by their communities. They often wrestle with this feeling alongside their own deep, personal identifications with being mothers/parents. Two of our authors, Beth and Jax, mention the role of the struggle for marriage equality in Australia as a part of the backdrop to their parenting journeys, reminding us that legal recognition is still in progress everywhere. Claire's story combines her passionate love for her kids as well as her conviction that they were meant to be hers with a legal struggle with her ex-wife and known donor for legal recognition of her relationship to their children. As Sonja says, reflecting on the alienating nature of the second-parent adoption process, these processes alienate nonbiological mothers from their own experience as parents, inserting the state as an arbiter for who really is a mother.

Alongside legal recognition, social recognition is central to our own feelings about parenting. Leah talks about always wanting to be a mother and being so excited when her wife was pregnant—only to have people dismiss her motherhood in casual conversation, as if only pregnancy matters. Nadja identifies as a comother, and even though she feels some awkwardness in the context of heteronormative parenting contexts, she approaches the world by asserting her rainbow family structure and making sure her family will be accepted and welcomed. Patricia discusses the way that assumptions about her desire to be a biological mother undermined her sense of self as a mother to her first child but eventually helped cement her conviction that she was happy being a nonbiological mother.

As nonbiological and nongestational parents, the role of biology and the desire (or the lack thereof) to become pregnant are a part of our experience of parenting. Several of the authors in this book, such as Melissa and Beth, had originally wanted to get pregnant but experienced fertility issues, leading to their partners being the one to get pregnant. These experiences can lead to complicated feelings of jealousy and grief but also to finding new types of joy in the experience of parenting as a nonbiological mother. Emily writes about deciding as a teen that she would never get pregnant, in part due to her history as a cancer survivor and her complicated relationship to her body, but accepts the awkward way she gets integrated into spaces dominated by biological mothers. Raechel writes about never wanting to be a parent and then becoming one through adoption; she discusses her own fertility journey that gave her a new understanding of the different ways to be a mother. In addition, many of our authors are both nonbiological as well as biological mothers, such as Louise, Stacy, Leah, and Sonja, but they still find that their love for their children is less determined by their biological relationships than by the love and work that makes up their parenting journey.

We hope you find these themes as well as the others you discover as you read this book to be nourishing and supportive of your own reflections on what motherhood/parenthood, love, and biology mean to you, no matter whether you are a biological or nonbiological parent. Thank you, dear reader, for joining us in this exploration of the experiences of nonbiological and nongestational queer mothers/parents. We'd love to hear from you—your stories, your thoughts on the book, or any other comments. Please email the editors at queermomsbook@gmail.com

Works Cited

Bartky, Sandra Lee. *Femininity and Domination: Studies in the Phenomenology of Oppression.* Taylor & Francis, 2015.

Honneth, Axel. *The Struggle for Recognition: the Moral Grammar of Social Conflicts.* MIT Press, 2007.

hooks, bell. "Theory as Liberatory Practice." *Yale J.L. & Feminism*, vol. 4, no. 1, 1991, digitalcommons.law.yale.edu/yjlf/vol4/iss1/2. Accessed 14 July 2020.

Pepper, Rachel. *The Ultimate Guide to Pregnancy for Lesbians: How to Stay Sane and Care for Yourself from Pre-Conception to Birth.* Cleis Press, 2005.

Chapter One

Little Arrows

J. Ryann Peyton

We named him Archer. He was brave and had piercing blue eyes. In the moment he looked at me for the first time, I felt my heart explode. He had my last name. He had my eyes and my hair. He was all of mine, yet he was also none of me. He was a stranger. He wasn't breathing. My wife was bleeding. The nurse said I had to go ... NOW.

Discovering one's identity as a parent is a complex journey. The impact and intersectionality of gender identity on parental identity is a topic most first-time parents never have to consider. As a gender-queer, nongestational parent, I spent eight months of my wife's pregnancy wondering how I would ever mother a child who did not come from my body and who would never know me as the feminine ideal of motherhood I thought he deserved. Yet when my son entered the world on his own terms, five weeks early in a blizzard at an altitude of nine thousand feet, my identity as a parent came swiftly into focus. I never imagined I would discover my identity as a parent in the neonatal intensive care unit (NICU). Yet it was the most perfect, remarkable experience I could have hoped for.

Our children choose us. Whether we create them genetically or otherwise, our children accept us based on the lessons they have to teach. In the first week of my son's life, he taught me that pronouns, gender expression, and legal status didn't define whether or not I was his mom. I was his mom because I held his feet for hours while the doctors worked to save his life. I was his mom because I was the only one at his side as he was transported from one hospital to the next. I was his mom because he absolutely needed me to be.

This is the story of how I discovered what it means to be a queer mom in the NICU. It begins with a handwritten note my wife scribbled on a nurse's chart to allow me to make medical decisions for a child the law did not consider to be mine, and it ends with the awakening of a true mother who is stronger, surer, and prouder than she ever thought was possible.

My story is one of little arrows. The little arrows of a gender binary the medical profession so dutifully follows. The little arrows of laws that tell nonbiological parents that they don't matter. The little arrows of strangers who question your legitimacy as a parent, a spouse, and a person. The little arrows of fear, uncertainty, and defiance at one's ability to wear their heart on the outside of their body. And the little arrows cast by the littlest archer of all who would never need my breast, my body, or my protection to survive.

Yet it was only in this death by a thousand cuts that I was able to find my true identity as a person and as a parent. Parenting can be a raw, eviscerating experience. It seems only fitting that my story of queer parenthood begin under a barrage of little arrows.

Part One: Target Practice

For many little girls, the pathway to motherhood starts early in life—caring for baby dolls, playing house, or serving as "mommy's little helper" to a younger sibling. The concept of motherhood is easily graspable to those assumed to be seeking it. I'm not one of those little girls.

I wasn't even sure if I was a girl. As a kid with a Zach Morris haircut and a propensity for wearing boy's clothes and underwear, the idea of being a mother never really seemed to resonate. When we played house, I always assumed the role of the dad named Kevin. I asked Santa for rollerblades instead of baby dolls. And while I was the oldest of four children, I was more interested in building bicycle races in the backyard than changing diapers or making bottles.

I was the quintessential "tomboy"—the label everyone else used to endearingly justify my gender expression and to convey their expectation that I would grow out of it someday. What they didn't understand was that I wanted to embody everything it meant to be a boy. I stopped wearing dresses and skirts all together. I asked my parents to call me by my middle name instead of my much more feminine first name. When they refused, I insisted that they call me Jessie and never Jessica. I never left the house without a backwards hat, and I relished every time someone complimented my parents on their son. Overtime, my tomboy label and masculine expression became more and more of an identity.

I reveled in this identity for years—confounding my parents, praying each night to wake up the next morning as a boy, and recoiling at the thought of being the little girl everyone else in my life wanted me to be. I told myself *Tomboys don't become mothers.*

My family moved around. A lot. Between fifth and ninth grade, I was in a new school every year. I wasn't great at making friends. I didn't look like the other girls. No one really knew what to do with me. The relentless loneliness of middle school as the new, shy, and genderqueer kid significantly informed my self-worth. My peers were pairing off with their first boyfriends. Girls started wearing makeup to school. The playground was a place for gossip and secret hand holding, not the dodgeball and obstacle courses I preferred. I got a "C" in home economics because I refused to bake and sew. In eighth grade, I decided that I was never getting married and I would certainly not have any children. Instead, I would travel the world and laugh at all of those silly girls baking cakes for husbands and children they hate. *Motherhood is for girls who can sew.*

Eventually it all became too much. My body was changing. Not into the boy I had hoped for but the woman I dreaded. Early 1990s sex education told me there were only two types of people in this world and their bodies only worked in two types of ways. No one dared give me any other way to describe myself. I knew women could be gay, but I didn't feel attracted to anyone, boy or girl. I liked being a tomboy, but I wondered what happens when tomboys grow up. How do they dress? How do they cut their hair? Do they change their names? What happens if they get mistaken for a man? I decided I wasn't brave enough to find out.

The world expected me to be a girl. My friends and family expected me to a girl. When I got to high school, I decided I would try being a girl. I grew out my hair, became practiced at making friends, and took an interest in boys. I let my mom do my makeup. I wore dresses to school dances. And wouldn't you know it, the sixteen-year-old girl who spent fourteen years of her life trying to be a boy dated the captain of the football team and was crowned homecoming queen.

After reaching what most teenage girls deem the pinnacle of high school, I realized that although I could successfully play the gender game, I wasn't going to be happy in the gender role everyone else expected me to play. This girlfriend of the football captain had developed a crush on the captain of the women's soccer team, and I felt increasingly disconnected from my body. College provided a natural end to the high school relationships and the gender expectations that came with them. Even so, my schizophrenic relationship with gender and sexuality continued through college and into law school. I would follow inclinations and curiosities like bread crumbs through a dense wood and slowly piece together a clearer picture of myself. It came at a price, however, as each new data point caused me to slip deeper into depression and anxiety. I had to get out. *Mothers don't run away.*

I met the woman who became my wife in 2008. I wasn't looking for a wife. I had moved to a new town to start my career. I didn't know a soul. I was still looking for myself. Yet in finding someone who finally saw me exactly the way I had always wanted to be seen, I also found the resolve to embrace my truest self. I had the courage to take on my more masculine middle name and to cut my hair again. I wore ties and threw away all of the dresses and skirts still in my possession. I finally let myself show up in my own life.

For the first time, I got to play house as me. And I began to truly consider what motherhood could mean for someone like me. The woman who wanted to be my wife certainly believed that I could be a mother. The notion of raising a child felt less foreign than it did a decade earlier. I knew I had the capacity to be a parent. But could I be a mother? Mothers are soft, gentle, beautiful, protective, and unbroken. I was none of those things. Would it be fair to a child to force them to grow up with a mom who looked and felt more like a dad? Yet if our children really do choose us, perhaps there was a child out there who needed someone as imperfect as me to be their mother. My brain was beginning to get on board. My body, however, rejected the idea entirely. If I was going to embrace motherhood, it would have to happen without my body's involvement. *Mothers are imperfect?*

Part Two: Archer

It is remarkable how we can sum up a person in a three-page list of traits from a donor profile: eye colour, hair colour, college major, graduate school, dust allergies, and so on. It is a bewildering experience to relentlessly pour over these lists in an attempt to find ourselves in categories of attributes we never knew we cared about.

Are blue-green eyes close enough to blue? Should allergies be a deal breaker? Should they be a lawyer like me? What about athletic ability? Becoming a mother meant finding myself in a list of potential fathers.

As is many people's experience, the process of making a baby didn't seem that complicated, and it was even fun at times. Sara was pregnant within a few months, and I don't recall a second thought ever crossing my mind. I took much delight in my impending parenthood. Every pregnancy has its ups and downs. Ours was no exception. Yet through each rollercoaster turn, we held on to each other and took each day in stride.

The due date was December 24. My birthday. I couldn't help but believe this was the universe's way of telling me it hadn't made a mistake. This really was my child. The days turned to weeks and the weeks turned to months. We had the requisite baby shower. I wore a tie.

The day after Thanksgiving we left for a "midwife-approved" trip to the mountains. We had planned a long weekend as one last hoorah before our family would change forever. After we unpacked, I headed out to ski for a few hours while Sara put together dinner. There was a storm coming.

As the snow began to fall, I looked forward to a weekend of fresh powder and many glasses of wine by the fire. We settled in for the evening with the first Christmas movie of the season and paid little attention to the accumulating snow and the rapidly dropping air pressure. Two hours later at nine thousand feet of elevation, in the midst of a blizzard, Sara's water broke. The storm was here.

After the obvious expletives and frantic calls to the midwife, we threw our recently unpacked clothes in a bag, and I collected myself enough to drive my now labouring wife to a hospital we never anticipated, on a night we never planned for, and in a snowstorm that seemed to be mocking me with every gust of blinding flakes. For the first time in the eight months, since I became a mother-to-be, I had second thoughts. *You have no right to be here.*

Our midwife and the safety of our birth centre were one hundred miles away down a snow-packed mountain. Not only did our midwife know our birth plan, she knew me. She knew my wife and I were legally married. She knew I wanted my name on the birth certificate. She knew I was empowered to make decisions for my wife and my child. She knew I shouldn't be excluded from these next few hours. The law said otherwise.

The only option was to keep driving forwards. So my wife, my second thoughts, and I drove into the blinding snow reminding each other to keep breathing. The quiet emergency room seemed inconvenienced by our arrival and request for swift attention. Paperwork. Insurance. Copays. Tunnel vision. Shaking knees. Cracking voice.

"There isn't a father. There's just me. What do you want me to write on this line?"

"I'm her wife. Do you want me to check the husband box?"

"We were married in Iowa in 2010. Yes, she is my legal wife."

"We have a power of attorney. I am her medical-decision maker. No, I don't have it with me. We weren't really planning on this."

"I fucking hate hospitals."

It seemed like hours had passed by the time they finally put us in a room. Our cozy mountain lodge was a distant memory, and for the first time since the storm hit, there was silence.

I walked into the bathroom and stared at my reflection under the buzzing, fluorescent light. My body couldn't decide whether it wanted to cry or throw up. Before it could decide, it was time to greet the parade of people coming in to let us know how the next twelve hours would go. Our doula had arrived from Denver. We had our support. Our midwife had called to convey our birth plan to the necessary decision makers. We had our plan. The doctors and nurses seemed satisfied with the liberties I had taken to make their forms more inclusive of our family. We had our permission. So I left my second thoughts in the bathroom mirror and returned to focus on supporting my wife through her escalating labour.

My wife and I have all of the same parts. Yet in watching her labour and ultimately give birth, I realized that her body was built to do something my body wasn't. In my heart, I knew that I could never be that strong or selfless. More than anything though, I knew that I could never ask for something so important from the parts of me that I had simply tolerated, ignored, or wished away for so many years. The overwhelming grief in that realization caught me by surprise. So there I sat, minutes away from meeting my child, in awe of my wife's strength and resolve, apologizing to my body for all of the years I had wished it was different.

As the sun was coming up, I glanced out the window at a beautiful vista of freshly fallen snow and a blue-bird sky. It was a new day. At 6:38 a.m., we met our son for the first time. He arrived a month ahead of schedule, but he was big and pink and screaming. They placed him in my wife's arms and suddenly we were a family of three. For a moment, my entire world was perfect.

I took in every wrinkle and curve and counted every finger and toe as his colour went from pink to grey. It was clear that he was struggling to breathe. Almost as soon as he arrived, they took him away. Without discussion or second thought, I left my still bleeding wife with our doula, and I followed our son.

By the time I saw him again, they had started an IV in his belly button, put an oxygen helmet over the majority of his body, and connected him to several loud, beeping machines. He was minutes old and already facing the biggest challenge of his life. And he was alone. *He needs his mother.*

We had barely become acquainted. I hadn't even held him. Yet there we were—two complete strangers in the midst of a life-altering moment. I looked at him, and he looked at me. My heart felt as though it might burst out of my chest. I knew that he didn't care what I looked like or whether I had a right to be in that room or whether it was my blood in his veins. He just needed to know he wasn't alone.

I guess when you can't define motherhood for yourself; the universe defines it for you. My first official act of motherhood was simply pulling up a chair. I sat at the end of the table and held the only accessible part of him—his feet. For the next two hours, we sat there to together. My hands wrapped around his tiny feet. After a long silence, I introduced myself. "Hi buddy. I'm your mama. Rough first day huh?"

It was the first time I had called myself a mother out loud. After twenty-eight years of angst about this one word, this one identity, it simply slipped out of my mouth without so much as a stutter. There was no audience and no fanfare. There was only this tiny person who didn't care what I called myself, so long as I loved him and didn't let go.

I told him how loved and wanted he was and how happy he had

already made his moms. I told him about our dog and all of his grandparents, aunts, uncles, and cousins who couldn't wait to meet him. I told him about how I was also born a month early in the middle of a blizzard. I told him it was all going to be okay.

Eventually, Sara was stable enough to venture into the room. We shared many tears. None of this was what we had hoped for or wanted. We held each other as we looked at him—this perfect human being that we had made together. We were all he had in this world. We had a short list of possible names but couldn't settle on "the one" because we wanted to meet him first. Once we met his intensity, we knew right away which name it would be: Archer.

No sooner had we made his name official, notified our families of the unexpected start to our vacation, and dealt with the logistics of having a baby in the mountains, the doctors told us it was time to go. His underdeveloped lungs weren't getting better in the thin mountain air, and the hospital, while apt at fixing ski injuries, simply didn't have the ability to treat a premature infant.

The storm that had caused Archer's unexpected arrival also prevented a helicopter from flying him back to Denver. We'd have to go by ambulance down the mountain. Sara wasn't well enough to be discharged yet, which meant I would have to go. Alone.

My second official act of motherhood was spelled out for me on the back of a nurse's chart paper. My name wasn't on his ID band. I hadn't given birth to him. I wasn't his presumed father. I had no authority or right or mandate to do anything for him. Yet I was the one who would be responsible for every decision that needed to be made for him in the 76.2 miles we would travel together on our way back to Denver.

The lawyer in me scribbled out a crude, two sentence contract for my wife to sign. It gave me permission to have access to my son and make medical decisions for him. We had the doctor sign as a witness, and I threw it in my pocket. I had no idea if it would actually provide the protection I needed, but it was all we had to offer to anyone who asked.

I kissed my wife and walked out the door behind our son. I wanted desperately to ride in the ambulance with him. To keep holding his feet to let him know he was not alone. But I was relegated to my car following behind. The drive was a blur. I hadn't slept in thirty hours, and I hadn't eaten in fourteen. I was alone for the first time and the sadness, fear, and joy of the night's events came rushing out of me. I'd never cried like that in all my life. For 76.2 miles I sat transfixed on the lights atop the ambulance in front of me. *As long as they don't turn on the lights, he is ok.*

I stayed behind that ambulance the entire way. When we arrived at the next hospital, we got separated as he was taken in through the emergency room and I parked the car. By the time I got to the emergency room, he was nowhere to be found.

Most people will tell you that I am an introvert's introvert. I don't even like asking for extra ketchup at the drive thru. Yet there I was standing in the middle of a busy emergency room frantically searching for a baby I had no legal right to find. *Where is my son?*

I didn't dare ask any of the doctors or nurses milling about out of fear that they would ask too many questions about who I was or whether I had the proper health information paperwork. I'd cross that bridge when it was necessary. Instead, I exchanged glances with a security guard who seemed to take an interest in my tempered chaos. His eyes darted between my hospital-issued scrub pants and my swollen red eyes. He smiled and said, "The NICU is on the fifth floor. You can take the staff elevator through here." Sometimes the universe puts the right people in the right place at the right time. I mustered a "thank you" and headed towards the elevator.

The fifth floor. A long hallway with a locked door. I peeked through the window. No one to be found. A doorbell. I was sure I'd reached the end of the line. I was convinced that the voice on the other end of the doorbell would be unfriendly, unaccepting, and generally unsupportive. The urge to run and hide was overwhelming. I pushed the button. No answer. I pushed the button again. Still no answer. My desire to run was suddenly replaced by panic. Something must be wrong. I could feel my hands start to sweat. I pushed the button again. Finally a voice. I'm not even sure what the voice said. I simply blurted out the first words I could find. *"I am Archer's mother. You have my son."*

The locked clicked, and I rushed through the door. To my surprise, I found a smiling nurse. "Welcome," she said, "he's right over here." She never asked for the crumbled-up contract in my pocket. She never questioned my right to be there. She simply took me to his room. I found him just the way I had left him at the last hospital, and I did the only thing I could do. I pulled up a chair and wrapped my hands around his familiar feet.

Part Three: Deep Cuts

When Sara arrived a few hours later, we were finally a family again. We both grieved our individual introductions to motherhood—hers ripped away in the precious moments after giving birth and left to care for herself now as a hospital visitor and not a patient and mine as the unlikely and unprepared coparent who could barely advocate for herself, much less a sick infant. We also grieved for him: the little boy who chose none of these things for his first day on earth, except for choosing us as his moms.

Eventually a doctor sauntered into the room. "Which one is mom?" he asked without any consideration. The day before, I probably wouldn't have given that question much thought, but not this day. Not on the day when I finally found the mother I wasn't sure was inside of me. Not on the day when every minute felt like a test of will and when every protocol and procedure felt like it was designed specifically to exclude someone like me. On this day, my identity, my role, and my competencies would not be questioned.

I felt my face run red hot and the tears start to form behind my eyes. "They both are," the nurse answered before I could explode or dissolve into a puddle. She directed an empathetic smile my way. I kept hold of Archer's feet in silent protest as I became the invisible "other" while the doctor made eye contact only with Sara to outline a prognosis and treatment plan.

The prognosis was good, and by that evening, Archer was disconnected from just about everything. Twelve hours after he arrived, Sara and I finally got to hold him unencumbered by machines, tubes, and wires. As we settled in and enjoyed our first moments together, the nurse returned with a new round of paperwork. I started in on the check boxes and insurance details and noticed the nurse putting an ID band on Sara's wrist. I made a mental note to follow up with her about how to put my name on the approved visitor list. But to my surprise, she asked for my wrist next.

There it was: The first tangible piece of evidence that I was a mother, and it was a simple plastic wristband with my son's name on it. I'd never valued anything as much as I valued that wristband. For seven days, we lived in the NICU. I never had to wonder if I would be questioned or denied or made to feel invisible. I had legitimacy and authority to be exactly where I was supposed to be. A week later I carried my son out of the hospital. With him, I also carried my pride and strength of identity as a mother. It was an identity I was never really sure I wanted, but it had embraced me anyways.

Motherhood for me did not require a gender identity or a legal status. Instead, it required a combination of love, forgiveness, acceptance, willingness, and tenacity. In hindsight, my entry into motherhood was exactly what was required for me to find out exactly who I could be as a parent. For once, I couldn't overthink it. I simply had to show up and be myself. Isn't that really what any type of parenthood is all about? We simply show up and give the best we have to our children.

Six years later, I have settled into my identity as a genderqueer mother. Sure, I never know whether to attend "Dads and Doughnuts" or "Mom's Night Out" at Archer's school, and no one wishes me a happy Mother's Day when our family goes out to brunch. But to those that matter, it is clear who and what I am in Archer's life.

We kept that handwritten contract in Archer's diaper bag for a year— always prepared in case someone challenged my ability to act as Archer's parent. Ultimately, it was important to us that the law recognizes me as Archer's mother. We petitioned for an adoption and sued the state of Colorado to legally recognize our marriage. We sought from the courts what public opinion would not provide to us. Ultimately, I did become Archer's legal parent. Next to the word "mother" on his birth certificate is my name. I don't need that piece of paper to define me, but for Archer's sake, I am glad that it exists. It helps both of us to take shelter from the little arrows of life that come with having two moms.

To Archer, I am simply his mama. He can't yet understand the complexity and uncertainty of the journey that brought us to this place. On the fifth anniversary of his adoption, I wrote Archer a letter—a coming out of sorts. Though wounded and cut and flawed, I am so proud to call myself his mother.

Dear Archie,

You don't remember this day five years ago, but I do. Your mommy and I had been married for two years. It had been exactly 389 days since we made you and exactly five months since I held your feet the minute you were born. I had changed over fifteen hundred diapers, lived in a NICU for eight days, lost hundreds of hours of sleep, and suddenly developed a patch of grey hair. I had learned how to calm your crying and how to make you laugh. My heart and my life had been forever changed.

But none of that mattered to the state of Colorado. Five years ago today, you sat in my lap while I explained to a judge, under oath, why I should have the legal right to be your mom.

I was never at a loss for the reasons why I wanted to be your mom. I knew I wanted you before you were even conceived. But even so, I felt unprepared to articulate my worth as your parent to a stranger who would ultimately decide whether it was in your best interests for me to serve in that role.

The litigator in me wanted to argue about the injustice of this day. The mother in me wanted to shield you from this day. The lawyer in me knew this day was necessary for the protection of us both. So I held you close and swallowed my pride and made the most important argument of my legal career.

We left with a piece of paper. It tells the rest of the world what we already knew: I am your mom.

Love makes a family, Archie. I'm sorry you'll go through life with an amended birth certificate and a court order because some people think love is not enough. But please know that I never needed this piece of paper to love you. You are enough.

Someday, you'll ask me to tell you the story of this day. We'll talk about the absurdity of the politics and the laws that necessitated this day. We'll talk about the tie we bought you just for this day. But more than anything, we'll talk about how we filled an entire courtroom with your grandparents, aunts, uncles, cousins, and friends and how on this day the judge put it on the record that he had never seen such a loved little boy.

You are loved, Archie. My most important job as your mom is to never, ever let you forget that.

Happy adoptionversary!

Love, Mama

Chapter Two

Big Little Love

Jax Jacki Brown

Anne and I met through an online dating app. I checked out her profile and said, "Hey, you're a bit cute." We chatted for a few days and then she got drunk on champers, asked for my number, and drunk called me. We had a funny, flirty conversation and agreed to go on our first date that weekend to a bar called Naked for Satan, which we now go back to every year to celebrate our anniversary. We've been inseparable ever since that night, but we didn't officially U-Haul until nine months, which we think was pretty restrained, although she was basically living at mine from the beginning.

After a month or so, we bought a tiny cactus together, which we christened "the cactus of tiny commitment." Now, that cactus sits on our windowsill and has spawned lots of cacti babies over our four years together.

We both knew early on it wasn't just a fling but something more serious and long term. I remember popping the "so would you like kids one day?" question on a cold winter street after I'd had too many wines. I was glad to hear we were on the same page, but it would be a few years before we would start trying to conceive.

***

You were our last embryo; our last glimmer of hope in what had been an emotionally and financially exhausting journey. We were ready to give up, convinced that you wouldn't take like the others hadn't. We braced ourselves for another negative pregnancy test, another awful clinical phone call: "You have been unsuccessful this month unfortunately. You are not pregnant. Sorry."

But you took! You snuggled into that plush home your Mum had built for you and you grew.

***

I feel it is important at this point to state clearly that I am adamantly prochoice and am in no way prolife. So it feels strange to write of our tiny clump of cells as though it possessed the consciousness of a fully formed human when I know that's not true. My love and connection to that clump of cells that grew into our daughter, Fern, was born out of the pain of going through in vitro fertilization (IVF) and of longing to be a parent.

I also know that not everyone who uses assisted reproductive technologies (ART) to try and conceive is able to have a baby in the end. I know just how lucky we are. Assisted reproduction is a multibillion-dollar industry. It is an industry built on selling hope to prospective parents. The industry sells the idea that if you just try for long enough and if you just spend enough money and submit your body over to the treatments, you will get a baby. This is just not true; not everyone successfully carries a pregnancy and has a baby in the end. There was recently a review into the ART Industry in the state of Victoria, Australia, where I live. The review suggested a number of key reforms, which included a requirement for fertility specialists to give patients accurate information regarding their chances of conceiving based on their age and presenting medical and fertility issues. Currently, fertility clinics in Australia are not required to provide this information, and the likelihood of success is often misrepresented to patients. Although the review was comprehensive in its investigation of the issues in ART and its inclusion of both patient, donor and donor conceived people's experiences, many of the recommendations for reform have not been implemented by the Victorian government. Of note, however, is that female same-sex couples are now recognized as one family when accessing donated sperm, eggs, or embryos. Previously, each woman was considered a separate family under the legislation and a donor could only have up to ten family spots. This meant that for many female same-sex couples who were not able to get two family spots, which was common because there is a sperm shortage in Victoria, only one woman was able to carry the couple's children. Additionally, with reciprocal IVF, the woman who was using her egg in her partner's womb was deemed a donor under the legislation, even though it was their shared child they had intentionally created in this way together.

***

Anne and I began our first reciprocal IVF round (my egg, Anne's womb). We were told we would get pregnant easily and I would produce lots of eggs as I was still in my early thirties. However, for reasons we will never know, this turned out to not be the case. In our first round, we got three eggs, two of which stopped growing by day three, and the last one was transferred into Anne at an additional cost of $2,500. Our specialist later admitted that our embryo didn't look that healthy and that it might have even stopped growing before the transfer. Why then, I asked, did she transfer it? "We find we have to transfer something into a woman each cycle otherwise she might not come back," she replied.

A round of IVF in Australia costs between $12,000 and $15,000 and that's if you forgo the additional costs of undertaking genetic testing. It's big bucks, which not everyone can afford. After our unsuccessful round, the nurse at our fertility clinic said, "come in and talk about options. We'll find something that works eventually"—as though we possessed endless finances to draw on and an endless well of resilience.

It's become so expensive because the industry is unregulated and profit is put before the people it purports to be assisting.

We waited a few months before trying again, as we were devastated by such low egg numbers and needed time to rest and regroup. When we began again, my daily hormones were increased significantly. I had nasal spray with my breakfast, and my nightcap was injections. We got four eggs, three of which fertilized.

We brought a bunch of cheapie pregnancy tests from the Internet and tested every morning as testing made us feel as if we had a tiny bit of control in a situation in which we felt very disempowered.

The day we got our first very faint positive, I was out at a meeting. Anne sent me a text: "I think I can see a second line, if I tilt it right and squint. I think I might be losing the plot, like actually. I'm coming into the city to meet you and you can tell me whether you can see it!"

We met on a busy street corner in Melbourne. Anne admits: "I did consider asking a pregnant lady on the train if she could see the second line but then thought that was too much of a weird thing to do."

She opened her handbag and pulled out the test, and we squinted down at it. She was right, if you turned it to the side, so the light caught it at a particular angle and stared hard, real hard, you could, maybe, see the faintest trace of a second line. At this point, I was pretty sure we were both on the edge of losing it. Who openly stares at a pregnancy test in broad daylight as people stream by?

After every embryo transfer, our clinic would give us a complimentary double pass to go and see a movie. I suggested we go to the movies to try and take our minds off if it was really as a positive test or not as there wasn't much point in testing again until morning. So we went to the cinema and headed straight to the accessible toilet for another quick look.

The next morning, the line was slightly more apparent and the following morning even more so. We continued testing even after Anne had the blood test to confirm it and the clinic had given us the long-awaited phone call. I think Anne ended up doing over twenty tests in the end. We just couldn't believe it! I even peed on a test just to confirm it wasn't a false positive.

***

We saw you for the first time at seven weeks! You were just a blob with a tiny heartbeat. I repeated the following in my head countless times a day: "Please keep growing little love, just keep growing little love!"

At ten weeks, we got to see you again. You were bigger, and your little heart was still ticking away. After the scan, our obstetrician sat us down and said she'd noticed that we had declined preimplantation genetic screening and wanted to let us know that it wasn't too late and that we could still screen the fetus for a variety of disabilities. She pushed a pamphlet across her desk at us outlining all the conditions they can screen for—Down syndrome, spinal muscular atrophy, cystic fibrosis. She asked, "Do you know what these conditions are?" "Yes," I replied. "Some of my friends have them." "Are they still alive?" the obstetrician asked. "Yep," I responded. "They live full and happy lives actually." Clearly, her only perspective on people with these disabilities was one where the babies die or are terminated.

When we were undertaking IVF, we were offered pregenetic screening on our embryos and were informed that all of the donor sperm in the state of Victoria undergoes testing for cystic fibrosis, fragile X syndrome, spinal muscular atrophy, and thrombophilia. Only the sperm that does not carry these conditions is accepted by the clinics. I did research and learned that two types of intersex variations—Turner and Klinefelter syndromes—are screened out. The "I" in our LGBTIQ community is being screened out, and those of us undertaking ART are complicit in this form of eugenics.

Screening for disability is something I happen to know a lot about. See, I'm a wheelchair user and my paid work and my life's passion are disability rights. My community is made up of fierce, proud, and political people with disabilities. As a wheelchair user, I know the value that can be found from living in a nonnormative body—the different perspective it provides me. It is not always easy, but the vast majority of what makes life hard is not due to my body being different but due to the disability discrimination I experience. This perspective is captured in the social model of disability, which comes out of the disability rights movement. It is the idea that much of the disadvantage people with disability experience is not because our bodies and minds are different but because society is inaccessible. In this radical reframing, being disabled becomes a socio-political issue of identity and a fight for equal rights, similar to the LGBTIQ experience. Alongside this structural discrimination runs the attitudes people hold about disability, as they often believe that disability is a terrible tragedy or, conversely, that people with disabilities are inspiring, even for doing nothing noteworthy at all. These are stereotypes of disability. I don't want to be viewed in stereotypical ways or have this story read as being inspirational. I want it to instead be provocative and to spark new perspectives and questions about how we think about and respond to difference.

What it means to live as a visibly disabled person in a world that is not built for me, how it feels to move through this world in my wheelchair, and the politics I've developed that enable me to navigate the world with pride and resilience instead of shame and sadness—these are all key things I want to teach my child whether she gains an impairment or spends her life as able bodied.

***

At the twelve-week scan, there you are again, beautiful and wiggly. The radiologist counted your fingers and toes and told us cheerily, "It's ok. They are all there." I said "we don't care if she's missing a couple actually," and she looked at me blankly. I was thinking of my outlandish and accomplished friend who was born with one arm and one leg and how she would teach you to be proud of any missing digits.

The radiologist printed us out a small photo of you that we took home and proudly stuck on our fringe. We affectionately called you "birdbrain" because the shape of your little brain in the scan looked uncannily like a hummingbird in flight. We excitedly did a Facebook pregnancy announcement—a picture of me holding up the scan photo to Anne's belly and clasping wooden rainbow building blocks on my lap. We got hundreds of likes. It was the middle of the marriage equality vote in Australia, so a particularly tough time to be creating a rainbow family. All of the major news outlets gave a platform for conservatives to say how damaging queer parenting was on children in the supposed interest of providing balanced coverage. So our community was looking for some love, something to be joyous about, and you my little love were it.

My disability community was really excited, too. Many people with disabilities are still denied the opportunity to be parents. A joint report by Disabled People Organisations Australia (DPO Australia) and National Women's Alliances found the following:

> A parent with disability in Australia—most often a mother—is up to ten times more likely than other parents to have a child removed from their care, often on the basis of parental disability rather than evidence of neglect or abuse. Women with disability also often lose their children in custody disputes simply because the woman has a disability (Disabled People Organisations Australia and National Women's Alliances 17).

Many women and girls with disabilities in Australia continue to be forcibly sterilized (Elliott 3). Access to respectful intimate relationships remains an area of discrimination for women with disabilities, and many still experience violence and abuse. "Women with disability are 40% more likely to be the victims of domestic violence than women without disability, and more than 70% of women with disability have been victims of violent sexual encounters at some time in their lives" (Frohmader and Cadwallader 13).

I am one of the lucky ones to have found someone who loves me deeply not despite of my disability but because of it and for all the richness it brings to my life.

***

The months ticked by slowly, and finally you made twenty-six and a half weeks—the gestation period when I was born. This was an emotional week for me, as I thought back about my young, hippie parents all those years ago and how they were catapulted into the overwhelming world of neonatal intensive care with my unexpected early arrival. Mum still can't look at those early photos of me in my humdicrib all full of tubes, skin paper thin. It would be six weeks before they would get to hold me, their little love, and longer before Mum was allowed to breastfeed me. I thought of them as you moved past my milestone and the fear they must have been consumed by and how this affected the parenting choices they would make for years to come. I wondered what they were told my future would look like. Were they given a percentage chance of survival? Were they told it was likely I would have some kind of disability? I haven't asked them these questions because they get too upset.

***

You were so happy inside your plush home. You'd grown big, measuring in the ninetieth percentile. Our little love is large! Your due date rolled around, and my parents turned up convinced you were going to arrive promptly that very day. You didn't, perhaps because your Mum loved being pregnant so much. She didn't want to let you go.

Our obstetrician let us go ten days overdue and then said we needed to induce and get you out if Anne was going to have any chance of the vaginal birth she had her heart set on. I won't go into the details of the labour apart from to say that it was quick, six hours, and you did, indeed, live up to the predictions of your size. You skipped 0000 newborn clothes altogether (all those tiny clothes we had painstakingly collected for you!) and went straight into the next size! You latched on to Anne's nipple almost immediately and ceased your loud protests about being evicted from your warm, cozy home.

Our midwife gave me skin to skin with you after you'd fed, and I snuggled you and rocked you back and forth in my chair. Oh, my little big love, you'd made it!

***

You turn six months old today as I write this and you continue to be on the bigger side of normal (what even is "normal" anyway?), growing and growing out of your clothes. I guess when I used to whisper into Anne's belly and into the ether "Just grow, just keep growing!" you heard me and didn't disappoint.

You have changed our life completely, as everyone tells expectant parents having a baby will do. You have taken over our life and our bed, refusing to sleep in your cot and squishing in between us. We now call you our little truffle pig as you snuffle in the night trying to find Anne's nipple in the dark. Yes, we are tired, exhausted in a whole new way. I am surprised at how much work I can still get done even on this little sleep, and there is substantially less "us" time for Anne and me.

I have recently acquired a LapBaby; it's like a big belt that goes around me with a little belt attached to it that clips around you. It means I can finally carry you. I can wheel about the house with you on my lap and read you books and show you the world from my vantage point. I take us on adventures into our big overgrown backyard, and we wheel up and explore the plants together, your little hands reaching out and grabbing at leaves. You love plants. We have a selection of plants on the bench in a corner of our kitchen, which we call your "plant kingdom," and we take you to them when you are crying, and they never fail to calm you as you look down over them. Your love of growing things makes us sure we have given you the right name, Fern.

***

When Anne was pregnant I asked a friend who is also a nongestational parent what it was like, and she said "it's like being the outside of an onion.... You have to hold the inside together [the birth parent and the baby], and make sure they are ok." I have found this to be true. Anne and Fern have their own intense thing going on with Anne having carried, birthed, and now being the primary caregiver. Fern needs Anne for breastfeeding and wants her for comfort when she's really upset, and I just don't cut it in these moments. I know this may change as she grows older, particularly when she's not breastfeeding anymore, but currently I am the outside of the onion. I am also working two jobs to support our family so that means I am away from home a lot, and when I am home, I am working a fair bit on my freelance work. This means I'm just not able to spend the amount of time with Fern that Anne does, so I make evenings and weekends count. Anne says I'm the "fun" parent. I get down on her level and play lots of games with her, and I am ace at reading books in all different, dorky voices. But it is hard. It's hard to be away so much, although I recognize I have a freedom, by being able to go out to work, that Anne currently doesn't have. It's hard to know that I'm needed and wanted less by our daughter. But Fern is growing and changing so much, so I know that this will change, too.

***

We couldn't love you more. You are so very loved and longed for; we are thankful you decided to stick with us. I am sure parenting will bring as many challenges as it does joys while we navigate the years to come together, but I am so deeply grateful that I get to wheel alongside you as you grow and change.

Works Cited

Disabled People's Organisations Australia (DPO Australia) and the National Women's Alliances (2019). *The Status of Women and Girls with Disability in Australia. Position Statement to the Commission on the Status of Women (CSW) Twenty-Fifth Anniversary of the Fourth World Conference on Women And The Beijing Declaration And Platform For Action.* DPO Australia, 1995.

Elliott, Laura. "Victims of Violence: The Forced Sterilisation of Women and Girls with Disabilities in Australia." *MDPI.com. Laws*, vol. 6, no. 8, 4 July 2017, doi.org/10.3390/laws6030008. Accessed 15 July 2020.

Frohmader, Carolyn and Jess Cadwallader. "Inquiry into Domestic Violence in Australia". Joint Submission from National Cross-Disability Disabled People's Organisations (DPO's). *Domestic Violence in Australia.* Submission 142. Sept. 2014.

Chapter Three

Family Recipe

Leah Oppenzato

Part I: Science

For as long as I can remember, I have wanted to be a mom. I was the kid who saved my pennies for a Cabbage Patch Kid and insisted on bringing her to every family mealtime, dressed in real diapers and my old baby clothes. I was immensely proud of the adoption certificate I mailed away for and which arrived printed with my name and address along with hers. I very seriously decided to keep her assigned name—Mia Kati—on her birth certificate so as to avoid confusion for her. My mother mentioned in passing that the doll looked Swiss-German, and I kept a notebook of *Schweizerdeutsch* words in order to preserve my new daughter's culture. I had pregnancy dreams all through high school. I finally adopted a small dog after college because my body seemed to crave an infant. I would never argue that every female is born to be a mother or a parent, but I have honestly always felt that I was. I struggled to admit my lesbian identity to myself, in part, because I feared it would put up barriers to becoming a parent and having a family.

I did eventually come out, to myself and everyone else, and met a woman with whom I wanted to start a family. When we began trying to conceive in 2006, the lesbian baby-making process still felt slightly revolutionary, somewhere between embarrassing and intriguing. But as I write this chapter in 2018, the story feels so ordinary as to be uninteresting: two lesbians and an anonymous sperm donor.

Once we chose the genetic material, we began the hard science. I am a gestational and biological parent as well as a nongestational/nonbiological one, so I can attest to some of the discomfort. During the journey to my own pregnancy (to create our family's second child), I met with many medical professionals: an OB/GYN, reproductive endocrinologists, my own primary care physician, and a midwife. I was given conflicting information about my health and fertility and was asked invasive questions that made me bristle, but what could I do if I wanted a child? And then there were the physical invasions. One fertility test actually made me feel as though my middle would explode. I had blood test after blood test, and more visits with the speculum than I care to recount.

When my wife became pregnant and we shared the news with friends and family, I saw sobering glimmers of the uncertainty of my role to come. I could see my role clearly, but the tiny slaps dug at my confidence. My wife always insisted on including me in any congratulations she received on the pregnancy, and too often she was met with responses like "You're the one who's pregnant!" Or "Oh, she's a dad!" Our medical professionals seemed to comprehend my role without questions and treated me accordingly. The reproductive endocrinologist congratulated both of us and printed extra ultrasound pictures for me. One midwife actually asked earnestly if our son's surprise blue eyes came from me, as my wife and the donor are both brown eyed.

Part II. The Law

The paradox of the American nongestational/nonbiological mom is the combined privilege and indignity of the second-parent adoption. At the time of our son's birth in 2007, the closest my wife and I could get to marriage was a domestic partnership filed with our city, which still left us legal strangers in the eyes of the state and the country. In order to approximate marriage and begin to secure my parenthood of the child I helped to create, we had to pay a lawyer to draw up a healthcare proxy, a durable power of attorney, a standby guardianship of the baby, and a form that gave me the right to make medical decisions for him. Yet even this shaky ground represented a best case scenario: my wife and son could easily be placed on my health insurance, and our state allowed second-parent adoptions to queer couples. The process was expensive, lengthy, and a lot of work but generally guaranteed a positive outcome. Unlike my easy experience adopting Mia the Cabbage Patch Kid, in our state, we had to pay a lawyer, pay a social worker for a home study, and wait for a court date. We started the process before our son's birth, and even so, we weren't able to finalize the adoption until he was eighteen months old. I knew deeply I was his mother before that, of course. But when his birth certificate arrived in the mail, I wished so fervently I could just mail in the enclosed birth certificate correction form, saying, "You made a mistake, state and city. You left off one of his parents. You left off the mama who helped choose his donor, was present for his conception, and dreamed of him since she was diapering dolls in elementary school." The correction form made pains to note that a woman who is married can add her husband's name to the birth certificate, even if he is not the biological father. The bureaucracy itself laid bare that it was never about the biology or intentionality of parenthood; it was about enforcing the status quo of heteronormativity at all costs. Why did our family have to jump through so many hoops to prove what couldn't be any truer?

In addition, I am Jewish, and my wife is Catholic. We made the decision long before conception to raise any children as Jews. According to Jewish law, children must have a Jewish (gestational) mother in order to be Jewish. We chose to convert our son. Conversion was less complicated than adoption, requiring just one trip to a mikvah (ritual bath) and a brief meeting with three rabbis of the beit din (Jewish rabbinical court), including and convened by our own rabbi. However, the range of Jewish law at that time was in fact far more flexible and forgiving than American law. Our rabbi, a lesbian married to a Catholic, reminded us repeatedly that the conversion was truly our choice. Even in 2007, both Reform and Reconstructionist Judaism considered the child of any interfaith couple to be Jewish, so long as the child was raised Jewish and participated in appropriate and timely Jewish lifecycle events.

Part III: The Crucible

Once my wife was pregnant, I took on nesting like a fulltime job. I chased down the best pregnancy planner and diligently filled it out, checking off boxes as the pregnancy progressed. My wife's response to this was "You're going to organize my pregnancy?" My response was

"Yes." I researched the most informative pregnancy books, obstetricians versus midwives, paediatricians, and daycares. I pored over baby websites and Craigslist, creating a registry and collecting used items locally. I even dispatched friends and relatives in neighbouring communities to keep an eye out for certain prized equipment. I washed tiny clothes and obsessed over which minicrib would fit best in our apartment. I attended every ultrasound and fell helplessly in love with my son when he was a bouncing jellybean with buds for limbs. I talked to him all the time while he floated around in utero. One unforgettable morning when I said goodbye to my wife's stomach, he kicked in response. I caught him when he was born and fought a variety of medical professionals to keep him in our room after delivery.

Those first days with a baby, in the hospital and then at home, passed in a blur with day and night indistinguishable. The world was suddenly tilted on its axis by eight pounds of tiny new human. We had a baby in our home! They just let us leave the hospital with him! I felt unqualified and unworthy but also as though I was finally doing my life's work.

During pregnancy, my wife ordered herself a maternity/nursing nightgown. It arrived with a teeny matching onesie. My wife thought it was tacky and ridiculous; she'd actually tried to avoid the sleepwear that advertised this option and was annoyed that the outfit was a pair after all. I thought the idea was precious and couldn't stop exclaiming over how delighted I was that she'd made the mistake and that I couldn't wait to take their picture together.

About a month later, for my birthday, my wife gave me a nightgown with a matching onesie. It was a maternity/nursing nightgown, which of course I did not need (although I ended up using it a few years later when I was pregnant and nursing our second child). The nightgown wasn't easy to find because there are lots of mother-daughter and father-son outfits, but no mother-son ones. A mother-gender neutral nightgown was hard to come by, but she found one because, she told me, "you're the mother, too." There were no questions about our family inside our apartment.

Yet when our freshly minted family ventured out into public, it all fell apart for me. Along with the congratulatory remarks, there was the bitter surprise of how unstable, unfamiliar, and often unwelcome my role was. At home, I was unquestionably my boy's mother. I changed diapers and found ways to shush him to sleep without nursing, and I matched his outfits and his socks and his pacifier ribbon. We had our adorable matching outfit. But I wasn't on his birth certificate. I didn't nurse him. I never really asked myself who I was to my son until the world started to demand the answer. My motherhood felt like both the most natural thing in the world and a daily assault against the world.

Everywhere I turned, fellow parents couldn't place me when they learned I was not only a nongestational/nonbiological parent, but fiercely unwilling to be placed in the role of lesbian dad. As we prepared to create our family, our path felt unconventional but not at all untravelled. I had no sense of beating back the brush on the path; on the contrary, I was surrounded by support: a well-established sperm bank that conducted research on queer families; couples in our neighbourhood and Jewish congregation who had used sperm donors; and a group of families who met via the Internet who were also in the process of creating their families in a variety of creative ways. So, I was startled by the stereotypes I seemed to crash into wherever I turned. I felt that I was supposed to choose between being the childbearing and childraising mom or the female dad with the more demanding job but who was never quite sure of the kids' shoe sizes or their teachers' names. Straight parents and fellow queers alike seemed bemused when they couldn't easily place me in either role. I immediately felt enormous compassion, sadness, and anger on behalf of fathers. At one early baby meetup, I complained offhandedly about the difficulty of snapping up a particular type of sleeper. Another mother said with surprise, "Oh, I guess that one really is confusing! I always just thought my husband was an idiot because he did it wrong." This deeply entrenched assumption that only women/gestational parents can care for children, even down to the snapping of their clothing, is so dangerous and harmful for all parents and all children and, ultimately is to the family itself.

I chose the mother name "Mama" for my own cultural reasons; the Yiddish "Mama" resonated with me. My wife preferred "Mommy," so the decision was simple. But I didn't realize going in that Mama is less frequently seen in American popular culture. The onesies read "Mommy's Little Boy"; the jewelry says "Mommy" in elegant script; even people on the street refer to a female parent as "Mommy." I thrilled with the few "Mama" references I could find, and I still wear my "Another Mama for Obama" shirt. That rhyme was like finding my name on a magnet back in the 1980s. This coincidence served to make me feel even more marginalized as a parent, as though the Mama I had chosen to be barely existed.

Parenting is such a truly physical activity that I always felt entwined with my boy. All of the carrying and cleaning up and cuddling, the tears and pee and blood and sweat, helped to do the hard work of knitting us together. Early parenting requires such an intense intimacy. I felt us working together to become a unit as soon as he was on the outside and even before, with his Morse code of kicks and flutters.

I know that I became a full parent to my (nongestational) child because not for a second did I feel that he was any less mine than the little girl I ended up growing in my own body. I worried a few years later as my own pregnancy progressed that I was displacing this beloved child by giving him a sibling. And I grieved at the change in our relationship when his baby sister was born and I was so often trapped underneath her. I was terrified that I was losing the close relationship with this son that I had worked so hard to create. I remember sitting on the floor when he was in the bathtub one evening, playing our silly game in which he made monster faces and noises at me, and I pretended to be scared. I felt a rush of relief that he still remembered our game and wanted to engage me and that this precious, hard-won nonbiological bond was not, after all, damaged by the biological one.

Part IV: Family Story

One way that you make a family is with science. Another way is through the legal system. And yet another way is with stories. I have, over the years, crafted the tale for our children about how they were made. Not just the science or the facts—although that part is extremely important, so they understand—but the feelings. The love we felt before their births. The intentionality and care that went into choosing their donor and the ways in which we were both full participants in both of their conceptions. The moment they entered the world they were so fully both of ours that the gestation was just the beginning.

We have also been honest with our kids about donor siblings. We are in contact with a few of the families who used our donor. We had the chance to meet one and have received photos and correspondence from two others. The children loved meeting their donor sister as well as studying the photos and letters for shared traits. These other people aren't members of their family, but all of these experiences make up their family story.

After reading the Percy Jackson and the Olympians series, the children suggested that they too could be demigods. Perhaps their anonymous donor was a god! Thus was born a new part of our family lore: brainstorming which deities might have given their traits to our children. Dionysus' party genes? Athena's wisdom? The impulsivity and passion of Zeus?

My son, now ten years old, loves science along with mythology. He has understood the genetic nature of family relationships, including the concept of DNA, from a surprisingly young age. He points out that "if you go back far enough in history I'm sure we have ancestors in common." My eight-year-old daughter enjoys looking at family photos and hearing about the narratives and relationships they represent. It is these threads and connections, just as invisible to the naked eye as DNA, that seem to inform her current definition of family. She accepts without argument that she is Italian because her mommy is Italian, and she enjoyed acting the role of her great-grandmother Angela on a family excursion earlier this year.

One day, while I was cuddled between my children, they began a mock fight over me. The eight-year-old asserted her claim: "I was borned from Mama." Not to be outdone, my ten-year-old replied, "But she caught me!" These sweet queerspawn have created their own narrative. I am learning from them how our family weaves together the sticky filaments of our DNA, stories, and simply love.

In the early days of my parenting, I was proudest and felt I had proved myself best when people forgot that I was neither a gestational nor a biological mother to my son. But I don't see parenthood that way anymore, as a contest about who is real. It's the Jewish law, patrilineal descent adapted to my lesbian family, that understands my motherhood the best: a parent can be neither a gestational or even biological relative but a person deeply entwined enough to give that child a crucial piece of their self. There is a form of the Hebrew verb "to birth," which can be used to describe the actions of both a father and a midwife: "to cause to birth." It is because the nonbiological/nongestational mother in a lesbian couple also "causes the baby to be born" in her own (nonbiological) way that she can be included in patrilineal descent. I did, after all, cause both of my children to be born.

If love is a verb, then so is family. It's something we have to make and remake every day, every week, across the years, even across the miles. I ended up a nongestational/nonbiological parent in some ways by happenstance. But I'd choose it again on purpose. I love parenting a child who I'm not connected to biologically and watching my wife do the same with our daughter. The experience has taught me so much about parenting, family, and biology, what all of these concepts mean to me as well as what they don't mean. It has given me the gift of constructing my family practically, emotionally, and narratively in ways that feel healthy and comfortable and loving and enriching for all of us. Love, intent, resolve, and commitment all connect us. I am so grateful that nongestational and nonbiological parenthood laid bare for me those deep beautiful bones that hold my family together.

Chapter Four

Redefining [M]other

Beth Cronin

When I was young, probably around twelve, I dreamed I was about to become a mother. I was in the shower and my belly was round and ripe with the baby that snuggled inside it. It felt real and definite—a promise and the fulfillment of my body's destiny.

Having a relationship with a woman was just not one of my life choices growing up. It's not that I consciously pushed it down; it just did not occur to me that it could be possible, even though I knew I was attracted to women. In my late teens and early twenties, I was in a relationship with a wonderful man I deeply loved. I knew I was destined to be a mother, and I relished the idea of our shared life and the parenthood that would inevitably follow. I thought I knew the map of my life—a relatively straightforward-looking road, worn well by so many before me. But that was not my road, and it was a messy, painful process to become the cartographer of my own mothering journey.

My study of cartography began at university where I completed my social work degree. This was a deeply confronting and liberating experience, which worked to deconstruct the well-meaning lenses of my sheltered rural life. Social work, gender studies, sociology, and philosophy shattered so many unquestioned things in my life and revealed unfathomed richness.

In my late teenage years, I started building a library of pregnancy and birthing books; I was already planning a gentle water birth at home and picturing the joy of those early breastfeeding years when I would be a true earth mother and fulfill all of my dreams. I believed motherhood would complete me, and now that I am on the other side of mothering, I can laugh lovingly at my romantic naivety.

In my early twenties, I stood at the beginning of the road I always thought I'd walk, but the map I had was actually never mine, and I realized love did not, and could not, conquer all. With less courage and integrity than I ever thought I could show, I ultimately embraced my love of women. Through the painful twists and turns, losses and grief, and the relief of authentic living that came with coming out, I found myself, but my map of motherhood was lost.

I entered a time of great exploration of the Feminine. I connected to some of my more pagan leanings and went on wild women weekends in Wales, swimming naked in lakes, and worked with some amazing women in England, which were profound times full of fire, ritual, and connection to Mother Earth. I explored my relationship with my own mother and made some peace with the ancestral baggage we all carry. I relished the preparations I was making for my own mothering adventures and explored the rites of passage of Maiden, Mother, Crone. I embraced every aspect of my womanhood, and I cleaved to the life-giving, fertile archetype of the mother I would be.

Early in my relationship with my now wife, I was ready to be a mother. My biological clock was ticking. Loudly. I was ready. My womb was pulsing, and my heart was aching. I was ready to fulfil my body's destiny and to carry that beautiful being I had dreamed of decades ago, and I was ready to be the Earth Mother I was meant to be. But our relationship was not ready. It was not even close to ready, and my yearnings were to fulfil my own, very individualized longing and desire to carry a child. I was not yet ready to create a family. This distinction has been the most profound and defining realisation of my life, and it has fundamentally shaped my understanding of love and parenting.

Years later, our dear friends sent us *And Tango Makes Three,* a beautiful book about two male penguins who fall in love and become a family when they embrace baby Tango (Richardson and Parnell). Our friends were able to name our fears and self-doubt and challenge the idea that becoming mothers was out of our reach. We looked at each other and somehow found the courage to dig beneath the tangled fears of not being enough and to tenderly and fiercely uncover our buried dreams of being mothers and our new longing to be a family.

It was important to us for our child to know their donor and to have a loving man in their life, someone to anchor them in the fullness of their identity in their world—a man not in our family but part of our family.

We did ask two men we knew whether they would consider being a donor for us, which itself was an interesting process. Through exploring what that would look like for us, for our child, and for the possible donor's self and family, it became clear that we needed to move to plan B. At times we still mourn this decision, knowing we might have made it work with our dear friend who offered to be a donor; however, I do wonder how I would have navigated the added sense of "otherness" seeing the inevitable bond between two people whose DNA has created this extraordinary miracle. We also wonder how it would have changed the dynamic of his family and our much-cherished friendship with them.

As we stand with our son[1] now, we are clear he would not be who he is without the donor we chose, and we are absolutely certain he is meant to be on the earth exactly as he is. We have the donor's photo up on our wall, and he is an integral part of our son's life story and the narrative of his life. We have started to make contact with the parents of our son's diblings (donor siblings), and we will support our son to the best of our ability if he ever chooses to connect with his donor or diblings in the future.

We both knew it was important to me to carry our child; this was unquestioned by us both, as this had not been a lifelong yearning for my wife. However, the road that led me to being a mother was full of grief and jealousy. I was to be the nonbiological, noncarrying, nonbreastfeeding [m]other, and this was incredibly difficult terrain to navigate. Our IVF specialist was thorough and skilled, and his message was clear but brutal, and we will always be deeply grateful to him for that. As it turned out, I would never be a mother in the way I always assumed I would be. I would never feel that little being grow in my womb, even though I was so certain from the age of twelve that she or he was somehow just waiting there. I would never feel my baby kick me from the inside, asserting their right to space and existence. I would never feel my body swell or stretch in unimaginable ways to create safe passage for my little one. I would never rock my baby to sleep in the moonlight and look in awe at how my body, with its mystical milk, can sustain and nourish with such perfection.

But I would watch my wife do all of these things. And this ache made a home in my heart—a cave where the wild wolf of grieving mothers dwells and comes out to howl. Somehow that part of me, that beautiful wolf, has become my wise counsel and the guardian of my broken heart.

She is the truth beneath the jealousy, resentment, and envy that sometimes rise up within me as I watch my wife and son share the closeness I always wanted, or those times when only the milky mama could possibly soothe his hurt or fear. The grief will always be a part of me, a scarred landscape that shapes the mother I am and the wife and mother I strive to be; and it morphed into something quite beautiful.

After our IVF specialist delivered the news that I would have a miniscule chance of falling pregnant and carrying our child, we both sat in the car park and wept together. We knew we only had the financial and emotional resources for three IVF rounds, and I do believe the decision to move forwards with my wife as the carrying mother was the moment I became a mother. My wife was full of grace in the aftermath of this crushing news, and she wholeheartedly and unreservedly gave me permission to say I just couldn't bear witnessing her become the carrying mother, using eggs from her body. The specialist described my wife's uterus as "perfect," and this was difficult to hear. She ultimately had to have surgery before we moved forward with the IVF, but her wonderful uterus would always remain perfect and mine would always remain empty.

Amid the tears it was very clear to me that this had, in fact, nothing to do with me or my narrow notions of womanhood and motherhood. This was about my wife and I deciding to create a family and to do whatever was best to give our baby life and safe passage. Together, we loved and dreamed him into being. I was more than prepared to do the work I knew I needed to do in order to become friends with this wild wolf of grief, and I knew my wife was more than willing to love me through that process.

Being the nonbiological mother has, ironically, shaped me into more of the mother, coparent, and partner I most wanted to be. It has been a defining part of my life and an incredible gift. My ego, and what I thought defined me and gave me worth and meaning, was an illusion. I was asked to surrender to my truest beliefs and to make a commitment to something so much larger than myself—this family I had chosen to cocreate. There is a sweet and momentous responsibility that comes with the decision to bring a child into this world. The ethical considerations are vast and deep, and the road is fraught with uncertainty.

Ultimately, this path to motherhood has been perfect. My wife and I have been provided with the unique challenges that each of us needed.

I have excavated beliefs about what being a woman means and have had to question my fears, my ego, and my unexamined notions about my identity as a woman. My wife embraced a new sense of belonging and love as she recognized her true place in my crazy love-rich family. I often wonder how much I navel gaze about how our child came into the world and why I am sensitive to other people's views of me as a mother. Why are social validation and visibility such powerful forces? I guess it comes back to our innate need for belonging in order to survive. The survival of human beings has hinged on belonging and acceptance from our community. To not have this is akin to annihilation; being cast out of our tribe in an evolutionary sense has meant death. Inclusion, belonging, and connection are fundamental needs we all share, and although in our modern-day lives, we can, perhaps, materially and physically survive being cast out, the impact on our spiritual wellbeing remains potentially devastating. I didn't want that for me, and I most definitely didn't want that for our son. When I dig deep enough, I also recognize a fear that perhaps our son would also see me as less than. I remember at some point in my twenties when I was considering children saying that "I just don't think I could bear loving something—someone—so much." And, indeed, the vulnerability of parenting is excruciating.

Parenting itself is a fast-flowing and often perilous river that can carve through stone. It illuminates the parts of ourselves that are etched in our subconscious: our character, our defenses, our responses to conflict, change, and fear, our comfortability with strong emotions, and our insecurities. Being the nonbiological mother intensified this process for me as I struggled to stand on the sacred ground of my mothering.

My adventure into motherhood has expanded my capacity for empathy and connection with groups of people I otherwise would not have recognized. I feel a greater affinity with fathers, which I initially found confusing and confronting but such a gift now. I have a better understanding of how watching the close and intense relationship between a breastfeeding-mother and their child can bring some chaos to the equilibrium of an intimate partner relationship and can cast the noncarrying parent into an unknown and often lonely landscape. I never thought I would be the breadwinner of the family or be working fulltime in the early years of motherhood. I always knew I wanted my children to experience attachment parenting, but it didn't occur to me that I would not be the breastfeeding mother—the physical foundation of my child's sense of safety in this world. We had planned and saved so that I could take several months leave without pay, and we were both at home with our son until I returned to fulltime work gradually. Our son inevitably found the majority of his comfort in the body of my wife—the one who every person on the planet already considered the unquestioned mother in our little family unit. It meant that not only would I have to navigate nine months of asserting my existence and my rightful place of mother while grieving for the experience of pregnancy; it meant that for years afterwards I would be—will be—outed as the "other" mother everywhere we went. On a Facebook group, a mother renamed the nonbiological "other" mother as an "also" mother. However, I often felt very much like the "other" mother, and all of my insecurities and self-doubts were magnified. I remember sitting in our sunroom one night, reading an article about the grief experience of nonbiological mothers. I wept and sobbed because I didn't think I could bear it. I wept because I felt so excruciatingly visible and so unseen at the same time. I wept because my grief sometimes morphed into bitterness and meant I was less of a wife than I wanted to be.

I also feel an expanded affinity for those whose lives have been altered by infertility and the unanswered call for a womb full of child. I've had conversations with others who have become mothers through fostering or adoption because they were unable to carry a child, and I have been deeply grateful for the sense of instant understanding I have felt. I can imagine the wolves that sometimes come out to howl for those women who have wanted to carry a child, just as they sometimes come out to howl for me.

When navigating this rugged terrain, I sought solace in books for lesbian mothers, although I didn't find my experience reflected there, as most noncarrying mothers went on to carry children and the stories didn't resonate. I also searched for my reflection in books for fathers, but I found that quite jarring. Someone made a comment once that likened my role to that of stepparent, which bewildered me. My wife and I loved this family into being and made every minute decision together. My existence was as essential to the creation of this little being as my wife's eggs or the donor's sperm. We both nourished and prepared the vessel our baby would grow in before, during, and after pregnancy; we agonized over the donor choices and every word on every donor document. Together, we grieved the first blastocyst that didn't make it, and I have been present for every second of our son's existence. We have shared every moment of worry and joy and delight and fear and every breath our son has taken.

It was, and sometimes still is, painful when people comment on how much our son looks like my wife. I went through a stage in the first few months when I told my wife and some close family members, "I don't care if it's true, I just need you to tell me he looks like me." It helped to be able to ask for that. We chose a donor who had some similar physical and character traits to me, and I love how our son really does look like me and how he has so many of my mannerisms. I love it when people can't guess who carried him and express their bewilderment that he can look like us both. I also love that he looks like my wife, even though I still sometimes feel a pang when people say it.

I was given a map of what family looks like—how to create one, how to nurture one, and how to create the ideal environment for a child to grow. This map assigned the roles I was meant to take and the choices I was meant to make. I was vulnerable to that map because I was marinated in Christian teachings throughout my childhood. I was vulnerable because I wanted to do right by my child, whom I knew I would love more fiercely and with more fragility than anything else in my life. But the maps were not written by cartographers who studied love or child development in any depth, and the terrain is so very different. The map was never a map. It was just an outdated blueprint of someone else's ideas.

Many heterosexual couples turn to science, donors, and IVF in order to become families, but their "otherness" is not immediately visible. I often reflect on the fact that no one would ever question my wife's place as our son's mother, but there are countless people across the globe who would question mine; in fact, there are countless people who would condemn me as not a mother at all.

Our son was seven months old when the conservative Australian government announced a noncompulsory, nonbinding postal survey about same-sex marriage (Stilinovic). The previous call for a plebiscite had been squashed, and I remember the depth of relief I felt at that time. It was hard to comprehend that the government of Australia would allow my relationship and family, my human rights, and the things most precious to me to be debated and voted on by everyone in the country, using money I had paid in tax. The majority support for marriage equality was already known, but we were political fodder in the global swing to far-right conservatism. I am very aware of homophobia and transphobia and of the daily microaggressions our family would face, but I didn't want our family or our communities to have to face an unleashed invitation to publicly declare opposition to our existence or equality under the law. As a new mother and a nonbiological mother, I felt particularly vulnerable, ferociously protective, and at the mercy of an unpredictable government and community. Looking at what was happening to LGBTIQ people in the United States and Russia, and the apparent boom of far-right conservatism across the world, I was deeply shaken. It made me painfully more aware of my own privilege, as this was the first time I had experienced government-sanctioned abuse, but I knew this was a daily reality for many other people. This deeper experience of my own privilege fortified my life-long commitment to social justice. It etched my own mothering manifesto into every cell of my body. It again illuminated the extraordinary responsibility I have in raising our son to be fully awake to his own privilege and to the systems of oppression that exist in our world—racism, sexism, ageism, homophobia and transphobia, ableism, and poverty. When I hone in on the magnitude of responsibility I have as a parent, the fact that I am a nonbiological mother becomes profoundly inconsequential. Raising our son to cultivate love, compassion, empathy, integrity, and a deep respect for himself, those around him, and Mother Earth needs my certainty and focus.

When our son was three months old, I was carrying him in a carrier holding my wife's hand through a shopping centre in the Gold Coast, Queensland when a large man turned, stared, and hissed at us. I wrapped my arms around our son and held on tightly to my wife's hand, and I hated the fear I felt. During the marriage equality campaign, my mum was having lunch with some women from church and they were talking about marriage equality. One woman said, "I don't care what they do as long as children aren't involved," and my mum was compelled to defend her grandson and the loving family we had brought him into. The debate was devastating for me. Every day and every night, it consumed me. Rage, despair, and hopelessness that first emerged when Trump was elected seemed to mushroom into an oppressive cloud. I came face to face with seemingly endless comments about how our relationship was less than, how we were endangering our son, and I witnessed the hurt and sadness of children from other rainbow families. I read things that were unthinkable, so full of hate and violence towards our families and communities. In every room and every meeting, I would look around and wonder who was going to vote against the equality of my relationship and family—who thought we were not equal and could now have a say about my rights and the things most precious to me. I felt humiliation and rage I could not have anticipated.

What also became clear throughout the horrors of the marriage equality debate was how blessed we are to have so many people around us who love us with such care and ferocity. We received rainbow packages of solidarity from across the world as well as hugs, texts, cards, and phone calls from friends, siblings, family, colleagues, and strangers. All were fierce and unwavering in their love and staunch in their commitment to equality. I was in awe as I saw the best and the worst in people, and the best shone so brightly it often made me cry. I am, we are all, indebted to the LGBTIQ elders and activists who came before us and who risked and endured much in this ongoing fight for equality. Indeed, we stand on the shoulders of giants.

From December 9 2017, marriage in Australia was legally defined as "a union between two people." The end did not justify the means.

I have always envisaged motherhood to be the greatest spiritual growth opportunity imaginable, and it continues to live up to this expectation. I also believe the greatest gift we can give to children is our connection to ourselves so we can be truly present, joy full and wholehearted. It means finding wisdom, humility, and self-compassion, and that is a lifelong quest.

I am so blessed to coparent with someone who holds such beautiful space for me in my mothering. Her story is as equally important and complex as mine. I imagine she would write about how difficult it has been to witness my grief and my pain; how the guilt has, at times, been crushing and has sometimes gotten in the way of her embracing the joys of being the carrying mother; and how the strong emotions we've had to navigate have sometimes ravaged the harmony we want to create for our son. I imagine she would also write about how we both wanted each other's mothering experiences at times and how when I left for work she would yearn for my freedom at the same I was yearning for our son to be more tethered to my body. I know that sometimes I created less space for her experience than I wanted to. In my pain, I, at times, resented the fact that she shared a birthing experience with all the women in my family and with the amazing mothering mentors in our lives, when I felt so alone. I mourn that I didn't create more space for her story and experience at such a crucial time of her own mothering adventure.

Writing my experience here has helped me to find a place for the maps I have created for myself throughout my mothering journey thus far. It has honed and refined my cartography skills and helped me to follow the tracks of the wolf and embrace the warmth of her fur and the tenderness in her howl. I cherish being a mother, and I love how my wife and I are together creating this flawed and perfect masterpiece of our family.

Oprah Winfrey once paraphrased a quote that holds much meaning for me: "Forgiveness is giving up the hope that the past could be any different" (qtd. in Podrazic). I'm not sure who I'm forgiving when I think of my path to mothering, but much of parenting is about the art of letting go, and in my more enlightened, best-self moments, there is pristine clarity that our shared mothering has unfolded exactly as it should. I also recognize that grief and letting go are inherent aspects of the parenting terrain. We lose so much of ourselves—our freedom and solitude, our sleep, our income and self-agency, our spontaneity and energy and ease, our social lives, our illusions of control, our lazy days and evenings and couple time... you name it, we lose it. And we gain the most extraordinary things. My purpose and my values have sharpened focus, and my strivings are more refined. My centre of gravity changed the moment he was born, and I will be eternally grateful. My son and my wife offer me my clearest reflection and are undoubtedly my greatest teachers and the loves of my life.

Somehow, I have gained more of myself in this journey of motherhood than I ever dreamed. This birth has been the death of many things in my life, and that has made way for profound transformation and love. I know this chapter of my mothering has only just begun. I know, too, that I have always been a mother. We are all mothers. We give birth to our own spirits, our own souls, our dreams, and stories every day. We are a mother to our inner child and our wilding nature. Each of us cultivates life and creation every time we breathe, and we all contribute to the mothering of those around us.

Endnotes

1. I want to acknowledge that my language throughout this chapter reflects the mainstream view of sex as a binary concept. I recognize this is complex and problematic and also that this binary and the social construction of gender have contributed to some of the struggle in my own mothering experience.

Works Cited

Podrazic, Joan. "Oprah On Forgiveness: This Definition Was "Bigger Than an Aha Moment.'" *Huffington Post*, 7 Mar 2013, www.huff ingtonpost.com/2013/03/07/oprah-on-forgiveness-how-to-forgive_ n_2821736.html. Accessed 2 July 2020.

Richardson, Justin, and Peter Parnell. *And Tango Makes Three.* Little Simon, 2005.

Stilinovic, Milly. "Australia is Having a Plebiscite on Gay Marriage – Here's What That Means". *Forbes.com.* 11 Aug 2017. www.forbes. com/sites/millystilinovic/2017/08/11/australia-is-having-a plebiscite -on-gay-marriage-heres-what-that-means/#3c2e87914347.

Chapter Five

Becoming Mommy

Louise Silver[1]

H azel, age three, was fuming, but I wasn't totally sure why. All I had done was gently remind her to bring her lunchbox up the stairs and inside after we got home from preschool. But when we got in the house, she had this snarl on her face, like something was bubbling up inside her and hijacking her facial muscles.

"What's going on, Haze?" I asked.

"If you're going to be alive, I don't want to be alive" she said, and looked away.

"What?" I said.

"I wish I didn't know you," she replied.

In that moment I felt like a child myself. I wanted to sob but reminded myself that I was supposed to be the adult here. The right thing to say was "I love you no matter what, even if you feel like you hate me right now." So, I swallowed the lump in my throat and said it.

It had been like this from the beginning, really, way before she could speak full sentences. People told us this was normal and that the parental preference would subside. They told us that it wouldn't matter that Anna carried Hazel and that I was the nonbiological mother. These distinctions would fade over time, they said. But as Hazel got older, it only seemed to get worse.

And it wasn't supposed to be like this.

I had wanted to be pregnant and have a baby for as long as I could remember, but settling into my thirties without a partner, I couldn't imagine how it would happen. Then, in a wind-battered tent on a stormy night at a music festival, I started a list of baby names in my damp and dirty notebook. The next morning, I called my mom from a pay phone to tell her my decision: I would be a single mother by choice. I was prepared to beg her to support me, financially and emotionally, but it turns out I didn't have to beg at all. "Okay," she said, surprisingly unsurprised. "Let's do it!"

Back home, my mother accompanied me on visits to the doctor, and I started having all the tests a person over thirty who wants to get pregnant through insemination needs to have—FSH and LH levels, etc. Everything looked good. I started looking through sperm catalogs online, and after a while, I found the perfect donor: Wyatt. He was healthy, talented, kind, and handsome. I sent his profile out to my friends and family to get their input. My sister, who didn't want kids of her own but was thrilled by the idea of becoming the "Fun Auntie," wrote, "I love him! Congratulations!" He was unanimously approved.

I kept an online dating profile up but focused my attention elsewhere. Predictably, it was then that my wife-to-be found and messaged me. When Anna and I went on our first date, I already had Wyatt's vials on reserve. I figured she should know this (why waste any more time?), so I told her. Talk about the lesbian U-Haul stereotype! But she wasn't scared away. She wanted to have kids too, she said. We liked each other. I treated her to lunch and said, "You can get me next time." When we hugged goodbye that day it was both kind of awkward and totally natural.

We dated and, after several months, moved in together. Our biological clocks were ticking, and it was less than a year after we met that I started trying. And trying. And trying again. First, we tried at Kaiser's Reproductive Endocrinology office, seat-belting the R2-D2-esque liquid nitrogen sperm tank in the car ride to the city. I wrote a song to the tune of They Might Be Giant's "Particle Man" called "Follicle Scan" to process my frustration with the unfriendly nurse practitioner who seemed totally insensitive to the fact that my irregular cycles made predicting ovulation impossible. "You could try IVF," said the doctor, after just three failed attempts. But we weren't there yet.

Instead, we decided to try at home, ceremoniously, with a queer midwife and tea candles and mutual visualization. Using pastels, we made a welcome sign for the baby, incorporating womb imagery. We gathered a support group of friends who were also trying to conceive, shared our responses to questions written on paper strips, such as "What's the hardest part of TTC?" and "Share a story about peeing on sticks."

After several more failed IUIs, I got serious about taking charge of my fertility, reading a book to that effect cover to cover. I tracked my basal body temperature, cervical mucous, and cervical positioning. Anna put on a headlamp and used a speculum and cell phone camera to explore previously uncharted territories. She was patient with me, slow and steady, despite my ever-increasing anxiety and obsessiveness, and throughout the nightly fertility fireside chats, grappling with such unanswerable questions as "Why isn't this working?" and "What's wrong with me?"

As a next step, I actually made a PowerPoint presentation of my cycle, day by day, believing that if I just tracked it better, I could figure out the mystery of my elusive ovulation patterns. I ate seaweed and Brazil nuts, avoided gluten and dairy and sugar and anything even remotely delicious. And every month, I cried when the blood and cramps came, still denying and lying to myself, feeling sore breasts and all those other pregnancy signs—maybe it was just implantation bleeding? Nearly a year went by, and I never once got to see two pink lines on a pee stick.

Then, the most awful and shocking thing in the world happened and changed everything. A few days shy of her thirty-seventh birthday, my one and only beloved sister, Sabine, died suddenly in her sleep. And I felt I, too, had been destroyed, inside and out.

Two weeks after this, in a hazy moment of immeasurable grief, I told Anna she should try. Because life was short and shit wasn't going to be good for a long, long time, so we should at least have good along with the bad—a reason to get out of bed in the morning.

I still can't quite believe that my sensible, down-to-earth wife went along with this. Maybe she couldn't say "no" to a person in my state. But she agreed to try. Once. Turns out that it was all it took. A stab of ovulation pain and poof, Hazel was conceived.

At first, we were both shocked and in disbelief. How could this slight colouration on a pee stick mean we were actually going to have a baby? Then, upon confirmation that yes, this was really real, came a moment of elation—a strange feeling to experience atop a mountain of grief. And then came the complexity.

The first year after the death of one of the closest people in your life is widely understood to be a living nightmare, but in my case, it was also, paradoxically, full of excitement and new possibilities—a baby, a wedding, a new house. It was thrilling to see Anna's belly expanding, to hear the baby's little horse-galloping heartbeat. But it was also a miserable time, for both of us, in different ways. During the first trimester, as Anna lay on the couch with a cool washcloth on her forehead riding out waves of nausea, I lay on the floor on the other side of room, slipping in and out of the various stages of grief. I was angry and heartbroken; I wanted my big sister. I was jealous that Anna was the one personally experiencing the resurgence of life after death and resentful that I now had to care for her, when I myself was on such shaky ground. She would go to bed early, and I would be up for hours poring through old pictures of and texts from Sabine, trying to find her there but ending up crying alone.

As Anna's pregnancy progressed and her morning sickness abated, things shifted somewhat. She crawled out of her own misery and was able to witness mine. We both tried our best to empathize with and help each other. And there was so much to do to get ready for the baby; it was possible to keep my mind off my grief and get into task mode—to shop for tiny impractical onesies and booties and to design a nursery. But my pain was right beneath the surface. Picture me breaking into tears at the baby store at the sight of a "World's Best Auntie" onesie, and then, sadness turning into anger, picking a fight with my wife during the car ride home.

I was aggravated by the situation I had gotten myself into and the many things I couldn't change. But I was also apprehensive about what was coming next. I constantly questioned what my role would be once the baby came. I imagined that another mother would be superfluous in the equation, a third wheel. Having grown up within the stereotypical nuclear family—a mother and father occupying clearly distinguished gender roles—I couldn't envision the two-mom family we were creating. Certainly, I did not want to be "Dad" as I had experienced "Dad" as a child—the activity partner, the breadwinner, fun and loving, but one step removed from the primary bond. I wanted to be "Mom," the nurturer, the home base. I wanted Anna to scoot over and make room for me. I wanted, desperately, not to be left out. But no matter how much she scooted over, no matter how much she reassured me that I was crucial and central, my insecurities persisted.

Five days before her due date, Hazel was born via an unplanned Caesarean section. The doctor held up this tiny, purplish, perfect baby so I could see her over the surgical partition, and I got to announce, "It's a girl, right?" (the swollen genitals were ambiguous) and cut the umbilical cord. They brought her over to a little side table, used a syringe to clear her eyes and nose, and then handed her to me. I placed her on Anna's chest for a brief moment before gloved and masked personnel instructed us that she and I would need to be brought to the well-baby nursery while Anna would get stitched up and brought to the recovery room.

Down two hallways and around a corner, in the nursery, they poked and prodded Hazel while I watched. I couldn't believe that I would be entrusted with this tiny fragile thing, that I was its parent, and that it was somehow mine. A nurse placed her in my lap and told me to let the baby suck my pinkie. She latched on so hard that I laughed aloud. Then the nurse walked away and there I was, left alone with this infant who was vigorously sucking on the wrong thing. And though perhaps we could have sat there together like this for hours, both content, I knew there was someone else this baby needed to be with and someone else who needed to be with this baby, so I reluctantly rose and headed back down the hallway.

In the days, weeks and months that followed, there were certainly plenty of ways to be involved in taking care of a small baby, and my fear of being superfluous was quickly assuaged. Hazel was a firecracker, borderline colicky, and it took all hands on deck to soothe her, change her, swaddle her, sing to her, and bounce her. Since we were supplementing with pumped breastmilk and formula, I was able to feed Hazel too, and Anna and I split the responsibilities fifty-fifty; each one of us was as sleep-deprived and strung out as the other, although only one of us with an abdominal scar and sore boobs.

But while I knew I was needed and appreciated by both my wife and the baby, all was not resolved. Even though I often had the magic touch, swinging Hazel back and forth so quickly that I pulled my shoulder out getting her to stop crying, I still didn't think of myself as an equal mother to Anna. Unfortunately, the reactions of acquaintances and in-laws only substantiated my anxieties. Neighborhood moms stopped us on stroller walks to commiserate with Anna about nursing strikes and sleep regressions, ignoring me entirely. Acquaintances and in-laws said unintentionally hurtful things like, "Oh, that's Anna's baby. How cute!" or, to Hazel, "Your mom [meaning Anna, even though Hazel doesn't have a mom; she has a mama and a mommy] loved sweets just like you do!" Perhaps I was oversensitive, but I took each one of these slights to heart, and they hurt.

And so, for the first several months of becoming a parent, I would only refer to Hazel as "the baby" in therapy sessions. "Your baby, Lou," my therapist would say, encouraging me: "Try saying, 'My baby.'" But the words felt awkward in my mouth when I tried them on. It was hard for me to call Hazel "my baby" because, inside, I still wasn't sure that she was. How could she be? I was someone familiar, even special to her, sure. I was up with her in the middle of the night, got covered in my fair share of spit up, snot and puke, and changed at least half of the poopy diapers. I loved her, cared for her, and sacrificed for her. But she already had a great mother—Anna. How could she possibly be my baby, too?

Hazel's behaviours confirmed and reaffirmed my fears and insecurities. As a spirited and opinionated baby, she would constantly reach for her breastfeeding, bio mom (Mama), thrusting herself from my body and onto Anna's no matter how much I (Mommy) bounced her and sang to her. As she grew into a feisty toddler, she used her words to make her preferences crystal clear. She could finally say "Mommy" at around nineteen months, but at two years old, it was "Mama only" and "Nooooooo!" whenever it happened to be me coming to get her from naps or in the morning. It was always, "Up up Mama!" and "No Mommy!" At three, she could obliterate me with sharp words of rejection, like those from that top-of-the-stairs moment.

I remember talking to one nongestational mom, a close friend of my sister's actually, about her experience with her youngest son. As a toddler, he had, apparently, said to her "Go far, far away into the dark and never come back." But by age five, he adored her completely. I appreciated this show of empathy, but, somehow, it barely softened the blow of Hazel's snubs and verbal insults.

I tried but couldn't hide my jealousy, which made the whole thing worse. It was as though Hazel knew she could manipulate a situation by asserting her Mama preference, so she would do so at every opportunity. She wanted Mama to come get her in the morning. Mama needed to be the one to carry her, to help her get dressed, to read to her. I would then, unfairly, get mad at Anna who would then, unfairly, yell at Hazel.

Of course, it wasn't all bad, all the time. As Hazel got bigger, more self-assured, and more opinionated, she and I also had a lot of fun together. I found I enjoyed filling "dad" responsibilities; I felt proud and connected bringing her to swim lessons, soccer lessons, and paint-your-own pottery and indoor play spaces. She was so intelligent, so artistic, and so athletic. I loved being silly with her and making her giggle. When unknowing strangers would comment on how much we looked alike, I'd reply simply "thank you" and bask in the moment of it, telling myself that although she didn't have my genes, Hazel was created, in part, by me. Besides, it was becoming harder and harder to tell which aspects of her personality, her whole being, were due to nature and which to nurture.

I also began to carve out my mom role. I, Mommy, began to do most of the bedtime putdown routines. I was the first to rush to her aid when she cried. I took the lead in learning about toddler parenting, reading books, and soliciting help online to find the best ways to respond to Hazel's "big feelings." I wasn't Hazel's Mama, but I was her Mommy, and that was something.

And then, just when things would start to feel okay, like I knew who I was as Mommy and was beginning to be okay with it, there would be another one of those moments in which I would approach Hazel and she would simply not have it. I was just not the one she wanted. It did not help matters that Anna was the one at home with her more and had, therefore, learned to anticipate her needs more quickly and accurately than I ever could. Feeling rejected by this child who was supposed to be mine triggered my residual grief and exacerbated my sense of loss. Although I was never really alone, I often felt isolated. Sometimes, I felt like a voyeur, perversely peering in on the intimate bond of mother and child. Other times, I felt like an awkward schoolgirl with a crush on the classmate who never gave her a second glance. I felt I had to try so hard to earn Hazel's love and affection and I would never be satisfied with what she was able to give in return.

In these moments, I longed deeply for a baby to grow inside of me. I dreamed of a baby who would love me most from the start, a child I wouldn't have to try so hard to win over.

And so, we began to try again.

We went straight to IVF this time, having frozen some of my embryos the previous summer. These were genetically tested embryos, and, so we were told, it was likely to work the first time. After three failed attempts, I was heartbroken, livid, and dumbfounded. Our doctor could find no reason for why these embryos would not stick. He said we could keep trying but might want to consider other options.

All of this money (much of it from my hopeful, generous, and retired parents) and all this fancy, top-of-the-line medical treatment, yet no one could give me a straight answer about what was wrong with me and why a baby could not find my healthy, strong body a suitable place in which to grow. How I wished I could call my sister and talk it all through.

Feeling depressed but still unwilling to give up, I decided to go back and visit Dr. Knapp, a naturopath, someone I'd seen in the past. Perhaps alternative medicine would succeed where Western medicine was failing me. Surprisingly, she did not seem at all puzzled by what was going on. Immediately, she honed in a genetic issue impacting my body's inability to process synthetic folic acid. She prescribed me huge doses of folate and other B vitamins over three months and then encouraged me to try again. If this didn't work, Anna and I considered that maybe she could carry my embryo instead, not a perfect solution but a possibility I was beginning to accept.

It was pouring rain, unusual for our area, when I lay in the procedure room at the IVF clinic for the fourth time. Anna had to work, so my mother was the one squeezing my hand. Though not an overly spiritual or "woo woo" person, she told me that she was summoning the lineage of our female ancestors and my beloved sister and that they were all there rooting for me. Afterwards, back at my house, I ate pineapple, took aspirin, and rested in bed with a heating pad around my feet. Within a few days, I felt nauseated, and finally, finally, got to see that second pink line.

The thing about finally getting pregnant after having wanted to be for so long is that I was so happy that I didn't even really mind the morning sickness, or the insane sense of smell, or even the hormonal headaches. It was wonderful to be the one to have food cravings, to start to show, and to feel the kicking inside of me. It was lovely to come home after work and pass out in bed for a half hour before dinner. As the months passed and we felt confident this baby would stick and would continue to grow, we told Hazel she was going to be a big sister. We read her books about "waiting for baby." She would have to stop jumping on me and we couldn't wrestle anymore, for now, but I promised we could start up again after the baby was born. I thought about how this child would be born with a smart and fun older sister, something I no longer had. It seemed like such an incredible gift to give to someone. I thought about how there was another heart beating inside me—where I had felt hollowed out with grief for so long. I knew that since losing Sabine I would never be completely whole again, but I started to feel close to whole. I wondered if this baby would have Sabine's precociousness, her delicate features, or her long skinny legs. I desperately hoped I would see her again, in some way, in this child.

Nine days after his due date, our robust, resilient son ripped me open and entered this world. When the nurse put him on my chest, the first thing I noticed was the shape of his eyebrows—my eyebrows. It was the happiest moment of my life and also the most physically painful. As it turns out, my placenta was stuck inside me, and I hemorrhaged, losing a third of the blood from my body. Once again, I experienced simultaneously utter joy and extreme misery. But again, I survived.

Julian was a trooper. He latched on like a pro, and over the following days, weeks, and months, I got to experience the symbiosis, the primary-ness that I had so craved, with this baby, my baby. I had no trouble saying those words, which felt true and indisputable. I was mesmerized by the way his little fingers gripped mine when I nursed him. The intense way he gazed up into my eyes—it was almost too much to bear. He calmed down as soon as I picked him up. I was the one he wanted. I fell madly in love.

Anna immediately proved herself to be a much more gracious nonbiological mom than I. She had wanted this experience for me and had hoped that this pair of pairs, this square, would be more stable than the triangle we had been before, contrary to the laws of geometry. My wise wife had anticipated that after having a biological child, I would be less jealous, more assured of my significance to this family. And she was right. Thankfully, she did not fear for her own connection with the new baby, trusting it would come.

It felt so natural with him, like I knew just what to do, like I was just what he needed. He was easily soothed, very different temperamentally from his sister. But I was also terrified. Losing Sabine had made it all too real that the worst possible things can and do sometimes happen. I felt a level of responsibility for this baby that I had never quite felt before. It was as though my heart now existed outside of my body. I often found myself ear to the floor by the nursery door listening for breathing sounds. I upped my Zoloft.

For the months that followed, we primarily engaged in parallel parenting. I would tend to Julian's needs, and Anna would tend to

Hazel's. When one would wake during the night, we'd call out "that's him!" or "that's her!" and most often, the designated mom would stumble out of bed to meet the needs of the child she had birthed.

If prior to Julian's birth I had been the crushed-out schoolgirl pining for Hazel's affections, I had now become desirable to her, hard to get. It seemed I was always nursing the baby, changing the baby, coddling him, and soothing him. What we began to call "lap wars" ensued. Every time Julian would crawl into my lap for story time, Hazel would plop herself there, too. "Why do you always give all of your attention to Julian?" she asked one day, exasperated. Recognizing that this was a normal, dramatic thing for a four-year-old to say and think, I also worried that she might be somewhat right. What I wanted to say in response was, "You never wanted all of my attention, or I would have given it to you!" But instead, I said I was sorry she felt that way and asked whether she like to have some special time. I vowed to let my uncomplicated love affair with baby Julian instruct and guide me to keep loving Hazel fiercely and unconditionally, too. I vowed to remember that she needs me too and that I am crucial to her, even if and when she pushes me away.

Julian is eighteen months old now and is becoming more independent every day, although my arms and breasts are still his refuge when he needs comforting. In our best moments, some lazy Sunday afternoons, we are a family of four, flopping upon each other on a king-sized mattress, wrestling and giggling, connected as one. Anna is lying on her back, holding Julian up in the air, bouncing him up and down just as she did with Hazel when she was his size. I've got Hazel flying at the end of my feet like an airplane, her arms reaching wide to each side, begging me to somehow get her higher, higher! The two of them have started to wrestle with each other, too, like little bear cubs, like my sister and me so many years ago. He chases after her, looks up to her, and emulates her in the same way I always did with Sabine. It is the most beautiful thing to watch, and I am so grateful to have been able to give him to her and her to him.

Often, though, we still find ourselves, by default, parenting along biological lines. Anna chases Hazel as she bikes across the park; I spot Julian as he climbs up the play structure. Anna reads to Hazel as she has her nighttime snack, and I nurse Julian to sleep. Everyone is mostly okay with this; it's just sort of the way it is right now.

But I also make sure to carve out space for Hazel and me to do our special Mommy things and to give Anna some time with her baby boy. I am teaching Hazel to read and can't wait until she's old enough to appreciate the stories that were my sister and my favourites, particularly the Oz books. We share a love of dark chocolate, playing basketball, and making sculptures and statues out of pattern blocks and Magna-Tiles. Hazel knows that I'm the mom who will break the routine and who might even let her stay up a teensy bit past her bedtime to watch a movie on a special occasion. And I often have more patience with her than Anna does, more understanding of her big feelings; I'm more open to trying out new parenting strategies and finding creative solutions to a dilemma.

Meanwhile, no longer an infant, Julian is beginning to practice his assertiveness. It's a weekday morning, and we're all scrambling to get ready when Anna picks him up from the floor to change his diaper. As she carries him to the bathroom, he dives towards me, kicking his legs and screams "Mama!" And I'm beginning to realize that this is just what babies do and that it wasn't some inadequacy on my part or some fault of Hazel's that made her do this to me the first time around. This is just what happens.

I now know that, according to all the research, babies and toddlers usually create a primary bond with one parent, typically the one with whom they spend the most time or who has the more nurturing personality. This is true in adoptive families and gay male families as well. I know that fighting against the dynamic, by insisting that Hazel bond with me in the same way as she did with Anna, only made her push me away more. I wish I could have explained all of this to my prepregnancy self. I wish I could reassure all of the nonbiological or otherwise less-favoured parents of young kids I know who, on some level, blame themselves for being second best.

As it turns out, Hazel understands all of this, too. She has probably understood it for quite some time, actually. Just a few weeks ago at dinner, our astute four-and-a-half-year-old explained it plain and simply: "I'll tell you a secret," she said. "The ones that we came out of, we like more. When we're babies, we just like the one, but when we get older, we start to like the other one." I guess that means she likes me these days. Looking back, I am aware that becoming Mommy to Hazel took a long time, whereas becoming Mama to Julian was a lot quicker. I imagine one day I'll just be "Mom" or "Ma" to both of them. Perhaps Hazel wasn't "my baby," but I have no doubt that she is now my daughter.

The grief of losing my sister and the trauma I experienced are still present, but my children and my wife heal me more and more every day. Though still a toddler, Julian already embodies some of my sister's spirit. I see her in his zest for books, his charm, and his dimpled cheeks. But I also see Sabine in Hazel, in her bossy big-sisterliness, in her creativity, and in her sensitivity. I know that if my sister were here, she would be so proud of both of them, and of me, for growing up to become a mother after all these years.

Endnotes

1. Pseudonyms are used throughout.

Chapter Six

Love Is All You Need

Sherri Martin-Baron

"I don't want to have special lunch with *you*," she says in the high-pitched timbre of a three-year-old. Here we go again: my latest attempt to spend some quality time with my firstborn thwarted. Ellie usually goes to Grandma's house after preschool, but I was hoping to spend some quality time with her the next day and had even reworked my schedule to do so.

Frustration and a slight sadness creep in, but I shake it off. I've been trying to carve out time just for the two of us lately to strengthen our relationship, but she can be fairly resistant. I do understand why she would be opposed, since having a lunch date with me is not part of her regular routine. I suppose it's a fairly normal reaction for a preschooler.

But here's the thing: Whenever we haven't gotten enough bonding time, she misbehaves towards me. Mostly, it's by not listening, but sometimes she kicks or hits me. I know she's acting out because she's not getting enough of something she needs—sleep, time with Mama, time with me, time with Grandma. It's clear that when she gets what she needs, she is happy, calm, and a better listener. When she and I do get quality time together, I notice that she is not only more well behaved but also more affectionate towards me as well and it lasts for several days. That's meaningful. I think there's a sense of trust that gets reaffirmed when we get that time to bond.

Since the twins were born, our lives have been turned upside down. Willa and Miriam are wonderful babies, but there are two of them, and at eight months, they are a handful, especially since Miriam is crawling already and Willa is on the verge. It isn't easy for either me or my wife, Michelle, to get one-on-one time with Ellie, and if there is time, she wants to be with Mama. Between the two of us, I'm never chosen.

In the mornings, I usually play it cool until Ellie is ready to initiate contact. If I need to go in to Ellie's room first, then I get the inevitable "Not you! Mama!"

People say that parental preferences change, but I have not seen that play out yet. What I have experienced instead is a slow but worthwhile process of increasing closeness between us.

***

I pick her up the following day from preschool, and to my relief, she is delighted to see me. I ask her again about special lunch. When she says "no," I say "okay," even though I'm disappointed.

But then I try something.

"How about getting subs at Wegmans?"

"No. I don't like Wegmans. I wanna eat at Grandma's," she responds matter-of-factly.

Routine.

I'm almost ready to give up, but then I make one last-ditch effort: "How about Friendly's?"

She doesn't skip a beat. "Okay," she says.

I check again to avoid a potential tantrum later. "Really?" I ask.

"Yes. Friendly's."

There were no veggies on her plate. And I let her eat vanilla ice cream with whipped cream and M&Ms for dessert. I never do this. This kind of food is a rarity at our house. But it was worth it. We wear paper hats with pictures of ice cream on them and play a game in which she is Peter Rabbit and I am Mr. McGregor.

"Give me back that carrot!" I say.

"I ate your carrot!" she laughs.

We laugh, bond, and just have a good time together.

Later that evening at bedtime, she hugs me and tells me, "I love you," and even snuggles up to me as I sing her new favourite lullaby, "Beautiful Boy" by John Lennon. I change the lyrics a bit to "beautiful girl," and she is calm and happy. I'm relieved.

***

I am Ema (with an "E"). This is the Hebrew word for "mom." It's what I call my own mother because I lived in Israel during my formative years and I chose it because that's what felt most comfortable to me. Ellie says I am her "Ema mom." This is how I explained things to her when she was younger. I wanted her to understand that I was also her mother—different than her biological and breastfeeding mom, sure, but still her mom. I understand that this name doesn't make our connection immediately clear in English, but keeping this part of our family's identity is important to me.

I grappled with saying that I was her mom at first. I usually said, "her other mom" or "parent" when people asked our relationship, and I still sometimes do. On pondering why, I have put it down to two reasons: The first is that I didn't want the presumption that she has only one mother, and the second is that I didn't feel comfortable yet calling myself "mom," even though I was doing everything that my wife was doing except for breastfeeding. These days I find that saying "I'm one of her moms" suits me better. Slowly, slowly, using "I'm her mom" is feeling more and more right.

Sometimes, Ellie calls me "Mama" as well. I asked her about this once, and she said that since we were both her mom, she wanted to call us both "Mama." I said that was fine with me. My twins aren't talking yet since they are less than a year old, but when they do, I'm hoping they'll stick with "Ema"—or, at the very least, come up with something creative.

***

It took us nine (yes, nine) tries with IUI (intrauterine insemination) and two different sperm donors to conceive Ellie.

Like many other lesbian couples, we decided to go with an anonymous donor through a sperm bank. We did this to establish ourselves as the sole parents and also because we didn't want the complications that we have heard sometimes come with a known donor. We had briefly considered my brother as a known donor but ultimately decided against it, as that would mean that our children's uncle would also be their biological father, which would be too awkward for us.

Our fertility clinic works with a specific sperm bank that ships all over the world. After searching through profiles online and purchasing an extended package including extra photos, an essay, and staff impressions of two potential donors, we went with the print model. Don't judge—he was adorable, and we hoped queer. We tried six times to get

Michelle pregnant with this donor. After six tries, we went a different route.

The theatre carpenter was our next choice. Michelle and I are both theatre geeks, so this seemed fitting. We tried three times with this donor and were about to consider IVF when we finally got a positive pregnancy test result.

We were going to be parents!

***

Through the full-length mirror being held up by the nurses, I watched as the top of her head, red with blood and squished to fit, made its way through the birth canal. Michelle was chanting like a monk between pushes—"ohm ... ooohm ..."—and I was in awe and overwhelmed with emotion. Doing my part as the supportive birthing partner, I braced one of her feet as she pushed, wishing I could do more. When our beautiful firstborn finally fully emerged, she was noticeably a little grey. The umbilical cord had been wrapped once around her neck and ankle. In those first few moments, I was both terrified and a bit in shock. Luckily, there was a stellar neonatal nursing team on standby. Our darling, little Ellie perked right up, and about five to ten minutes later, she had a normal Apgar score.

I got to be there in the nursery when she was first being weighed and measured. I was the first person to hold her hand. As her tiny hand grasped my finger, I knew I was in love.

***

Becoming a parent for the first time changes everything, more than I ever could have anticipated. My relationships with my parents and in-laws changed; my relationship with myself, my relationship with my wife, and my relationship to the world changed as well. It was a life-altering and earth-shaking event.

It shouldn't have come as a surprise, then, that soon after Ellie was born, all of those intense and rapid changes started taking a toll. I started having compulsive thoughts. I have no official diagnosis, so these can be vaguely described as OCD-like in nature. Because this had never happened to me before, I had nothing to compare it to. I felt like I was going crazy, but I held on to the idea that I probably wasn't—or, at least, that I might be able to will these thoughts away. Mind over... well, mind.

The changes in our lives after Ellie's birth were so great and my stress level so high that these thoughts would enter my mind without permission. This happened only when the baby cried a certain way, and I still have no idea why. I would find myself randomly staring into space around the house listening to these renegade thoughts, not sure what to do and willing them to go away. This lasted several months.

Perhaps they came because I was stressed. At the time, I didn't have a steady job. I had been adjuncting for several years as an instructor teaching English to speakers of other languages. By chance, I had three job interviews when Ellie was between two and three weeks old; one was an eight-hour-long on-campus interview. I didn't get the job. I didn't get any of them. Now that we were three, I knew that I needed a steady job and income more than ever before. I felt like I was failing my new family.

Additionally, as the nonbreastfeeding parent of a child who never took a bottle (never!) and was now back at work, I had to consciously make sure that I was getting quality time with Ellie. One day when she was about four months old, Ellie wouldn't even look at me before I left for work, an hour-long commute each way. I was so distressed that I cried because I was going to be gone most of the day and didn't know when we would have a chance to connect.

Frequently during her first year, I struggled with feeling unwanted by Ellie. I was clearly the nonpreferred parent. We are much closer now, but I still play second fiddle to my wife. At least now I know how to manage my feelings about it (thanks to some articles on child psychology and, of course, therapy).

All of these factors likely contributed to those postpartum compulsive thoughts I was experiencing at this time. I kept this all to myself until they had subsided. The first person I told was my wife but not until a year later. As I was going through it, I was sure that these compulsive thoughts were connected to the stress and exhaustion of being a first time parent as well as the enormity of my world changing so drastically and that they would pass. Luckily, as I was going through it, I could rationalize that I was not going crazy and was hopeful that it would get better.

It did.

***

Once these internal stressors subsided, there was an outside stressor that loomed large: second-parent adoption.

It seemed insane to me since I was already listed as "mother" on her birth certificate (thank you, New York State). However, we got advice from many people and from our lawyer that a second-parent adoption was necessary. Consider these circumstances. We are traveling overseas and get rerouted to a non-LGBTQ friendly location. States start to strip away marriage rights the way abortion rights have been. And the list goes on. Our lawyer said it plainly and best when she stated, "Marriage rights aren't parental rights." And so we did it to protect our family.

The second-parent adoption process took an entire year and cost us $1,500. I had mixed feelings about the entire process. Both Michelle and I had to provide addresses for where we had lived for the previous twenty-eight years (not an easy task) and had to get fingerprinted. When I found out that the judge had ordered a social worker to come visit us, I sat down on the loveseat in our living room and cried.

"I just feel so... insulted!" I sobbed to our lawyer.

"I know. I went through it, too," she comforted.

It's pretty great to have a lawyer who is also a queer nonbiological mom like me right here in our small community.

The social worker turned out to be a lovely person but didn't understand why I was doing the adoption, since Michelle and I were married when we had Ellie. We explained, answered all of her questions honestly, and she gave us a glowing recommendation. On the day of the adoption, we decided to celebrate and got all dressed up. The judge was nice and gave Ellie a teddy bear. My mother-in-law came along for support.

It was worth it.

***

After about eighteen months, we started talking about having a second child. Personally, I wanted a second child because I have a brother with whom I'm very close. Although we fought like cats and dogs as children, as adults, we've grown close and are actually a lot alike. I know some very well-adjusted only-children as well as some siblings who are estranged from one another. But my own experience told me that it was important for our family to expand, and both my wife and I wanted it to. We also felt strongly that our child should grow up with others like her—that is, donor-conceived kids.

But I wasn't ready. Not yet.

I was afraid that the compulsive thoughts I had after Ellie was born would rear their ugly head once more.

***

So, how did we end up with a second (and third) child?

The turning point came over lunch one day when I finally told a work friend whom I trusted about my postpartum experience. I was testing the waters. I hadn't planned to talk about it, but she asked me about trying for more children, and it just came out. Just sharing about it, even without giving details, gave me the push that I needed to finally seek out therapy. I hadn't done so earlier for a variety of reasons. First, I had no name for what I was experiencing (and still don't). Second, I don't live in an area with an abundance of resources specifically for LGBTQ folk, and, third, I wasn't sure how seriously I would be taken as a nonbiological and nongestational parent complaining about postpartum issues, since our collective voices have been largely unseen or dismissed in this area.[1] Thankfully, my therapist believed my experience and was a willing support.

After telling my wife and going to therapy, I felt like I had the resources in place if this were to happen again. I finally felt ready to expand our family. We decided to try for a second child right before our firstborn turned two and went back to our favourite jolly doctor at the fertility clinic about an hour away. We expected that the process may take a while, since it took us so long to get Ellie. But to our great surprise and delight, it only took one try!

At our seven-week ultrasound, at the very moment when the monitor showed two gestational sacs, I screamed. The doctor responded by saying, "Hold on. I'm looking for more." I nearly fainted.

We were having twins!

"Two for the price of one," people say.

"Literally," I say. Sperm is expensive.

***

Parental preference hasn't been an issue with the twins—at least, so far. Michelle breastfeeds; I don't. Otherwise, we both do everything else, although Michelle does get up more frequently in the night. They take a bottle (Miriam prefers a sippy cup) and can even feed themselves now. I think that because there are two of them, they just haven't had the same experience that a singleton firstborn would have had; therefore, they seem more open to me as their parent. They are both smiley, happy babies, and neither has ever actively avoided me.

And even if that happens, it will be okay. There's just so much less stress since we've been through this before. Yes, even with twins the second time around, I have to say that becoming a parent for the first time was a much more difficult transition.

***

"Hi BFF. How r u?" texts my closest childhood friend the other night. We regularly check in with each other.

"Hi! I'm okay, but exhausted. I keep falling asleep randomly, like when Ellie and I were playing with slime tonight. I just had to lie down in her bed for a brief moment because I couldn't sit or stand up anymore! LOL! I was up four or five times with Willa last night between 2:00 and 6:00 a.m.! Ugh. Now I have to go lesson plan for tomorrow and hopefully shower because Miriam peed on me earlier during bath time."

Yup. This is my life now with three.

It's pretty great, actually.

***

Tonight, at bedtime, I tucked Ellie in and lay down next to her to help her calm down from an exciting day. She had gone swimming with Sabba and Savta, her grandparents on my side, who are visiting from out of town, and then we all had a yummy Shabbat dinner together at Grandma's, Michelle's mom's house.

Head on her pillow, Ellie looked at me, smiling, her big brown eyes staring into mine. As we looked at one another, a peaceful tranquility radiated between us. Then, to my surprise, she said softly, "We've done this before."

"You remember?" I replied tenderly and smiled back.

She didn't respond, so I reminded her. "We did this while Mama was in the hospital when the babies were born. I'd lie down with you to help you fall asleep ... and sometimes I fell asleep, too!"

Somewhere, I believe, she must remember that feeling if not the actual event.

I tucked her in and sang two of her favourite lullabies. Then I gave her a giant hug.

"Goodnight, my love," I whispered as I left the room.

And instead of her usual resistant "I'm *not* love," she simply said, "Goodnight."

It's moments like these that I live for as a mom—that connection and that peacefulness.

"All you need is love," the song says.

Too true.

Endnotes

1. I'd like to thank Michelle Loheac for her help with the wording of this situation.

Chapter Seven

Vinzi Is the Name of My Son

Nadja Miko-Schefzig

While I am writing this article, my little son is sound asleep and I am watching over him. We are currently spending two months in the north of England. My partner, Katharina, his biological mom, has a fellowship here at the university, and I am caring for him. It works well for me because summer is not a busy period in my field of work as a management consultant, and when there is something to do, I can do it here in the home office.

Today is Tuesday. When Vinzi wakes up, we'll sit on the windowsill and wait for the English garbage collection truck. They come here in a two-week alternating rhythm at approximately half-past ten. In Vienna, the residual waste collection comes on Monday, the biological waste collection on Friday. Our time table has now adapted to the new garbage disposal process because Vinzi is a fan of the orange trucks and the black cans with their differently coloured lids, and he loves to observe the guys who empty them. As soon as we see the garbage truck, I'll put Bruno, our Bernese mountain dog, on the leash and we'll hurry out and follow the garbage collectors through the whole village. We'll watch how it goes—in Vinzent's words—"bumbum" when the garbage containers are lifted and emptied onto the truck. That continues to be a favourite indoor game for the whole family as well; Vinzi can turn any object into an imagined garbage container, but, of course, we also have lifelike replica garbage trucks and containers. Vinzi currently also loves train games, cake baking, scooter driving, throwing stones into the water, and playing sand games. Not far from here, there are beautiful North Sea beaches with wide dune shores, where our entire rainbow family spends idyllic Sundays.

Vinzi is now three and a half years old. I've been his favourite mom for about three quarters of a year now. What does that mean? It means I'm supposed to sleep next to him, sit in front of him in the car, and make him his evening milk bottles. If I go away for a short time, he'll freak out quite a bit. I have no idea why it is like this right now. Is it part of his defiance phase? Is it because of partnership troubles between Katharina and me, or do I stand for a certain value he needs right now? When he was a little baby and he was focused on Katharina, it was innocent. It all happened directly out of a specific need, the need for eating, for sleeping, for playing. Now he can be very specific and differentiated and sometimes very hurtful to Katharina, as he expresses that he wants to have me—at least for the moment. How about if it were the other way around? I think we might have projected that onto my comotherhood and on the fact that we are not a normal hetero family or that I am the comother.

I'm flattered and worried because it strains my relationship with Katharina. It's terrible to be the second-best mother. For me, it was that way at the beginning, starting a few weeks after his birth, when Katharina had recovered from her Caesarean section and could take care of him. Katharina was on parental leave, breastfed Vinzent, and they slept together on their bedside. I was also important to him and walked around with him on my arm many nights when he could not sleep or when he woke up at four or five in the morning and I could do the early shift before work. Nevertheless, Katharina was the centre of his life, and he was hers. I was excluded, and the entire transformation of our relationship system from couple to small family was enormously frightening, unexpected, and stressful. I felt lonely and exhausted, had no time for myself and wanted to take care of everyone and everything— the work at my company, our baby when I came home, and the household that, from my perspective, Katharina could not also manage besides the baby. It was a terrible time, and we have still not gotten over it.

Today, I'm closer to Vinzent—at least now, at this stage of his development as a three-year-old. Will it stay that way or is it just a phase? Will he someday be ashamed of having me instead of a dad? Will he have to defend his rainbow family against discriminatory attacks? Or will he blame us for not having a father figure in his life? As generous as Katharina is with Vinzi concerning my role, it is important to her that she is the biological mom. What does that mean to her? What is or will be the difference between her and my role apart from our individual and personal diversity? It is ambiguous, but, then again, does it really matter to me? We will see, or as we say for reassurance in various crisis situations since Vinzent's birth—we will cross this bridge when we are there.

The first years of baby and work and relationship were really tough. It was less that I accepted the comother role as that I was catapulted into it. I started to do exactly what I couldn't stand about mothers in general. To be entirely self-sacrificing, I was a spinning top that had to stay focused, stay awake, get dressed and look spotless, be punctual at every appointment, and still come to grips with how the love of this new being, who was suddenly my child, grasped and seized me. At the same time, I was realizing how all of those stupid commonplaces about parenting apply to me—that you really do love your child more than yourself. But I have learned at least one lesson: I no longer judge others as easily as before. Motherhood, or rather comotherhood, has made me humbler because I often see what I am doing is wrong or at least imperfect and yet I cannot help it.

Our child calls me Mami and Katharina, Mama. Katharina made the decision to do it that way. I would have rather had it the other way around, but I could not prevail. Mama seemed to fit me better, as I am the taller and heavier mother of both of us and as Mami is a diminutive in German. But I have adapted pretty well to Mami; it sounds happy and playful to me now. So, I fill out the Mami role today, or, rather, I am trying to make myself fit into it.

When Katharina was already very pregnant in February 2015, we registered our partnership. This possibility has existed in Austria since 2010, but only since 2015 has there been the legal option that comothers may adopt their children and are, thus, legally equal to a biological parent. In this sense, Vinzi chose a perfect time for coming into the world because I could adopt him right away and was even allowed to receive parental leave benefits. We all have a common double name; even our dog Bruno is registered with it at the vet. The double name for children is another possibility that was only legalized in Austria in 2015, and that gives me a lot of security. I hardly ever have to worry that I would have trouble with any officials or at any border if I were to travel alone with Vinzi. In fact, we have hardly experienced any problems or discrimination as a rainbow family so far. We have been treated in a friendly and professional manner in all hospitals, at all children's courses, and all childcare facilities we've ever attended.

There have been irritations sometimes, but, in general, they have not affected us. The one time we really felt them was at a birth preparation course. There were seven couples, and Katharina and I, of course, were the only two-woman couple. The course was also led by a heterosexual couple, and, occasionally, we were divided for certain exercises or reflections into women and men. When that happened, I was allowed to choose if I wanted to go with the mothers or the fathers. I usually went to the fathers because I saw myself in the role of a supporter in giving birth and, thus, closer to the father's roles. At the end of the course, the fathers were told that after the birth of their babies, they could come every Saturday to a fathers' group. The organizer of this group then apologized to me and said that I was not allowed to participate in the fathers' group because, in his view, I did not fit and the fathers would behave differently if a woman were part of it. This was very painful for me in retrospect because I needed this group at the beginning. But apart from this explicit exclusionary experience, we, and explicitly I as a comother, have been treated by doctors, nurses, midwives, and childcare providers in courteous, friendly, and egalitarian manner, although pregnant women couples in Austria are certainly not yet on the daily agenda of certain institutions.

We read a lot of children's books to Vinzi, and most of them include a mom and quite often a mom and a dad. (Occasionally when I'm reading aloud, I will call the mother "Mommy" instead of "Mom.") So far, Vinzi has not asked why he actually has a mom and a mommy and not a mom and a dad like many of his children friends and many of the protagonists in his books and films. I hardly know any other comothers, at least not very well. It would be possible to find and meet other comoms in Vienna, since there has been a rainbow family group for some time now. Twice, we went to their meetings, which were nice, but it was exhausting and felt a bit artificial, too. Everything in our lives has become pragmatic and I try to keep things as simple and easy as possible, so we have to make choices based on our priorities. In the end, my need to know other comothers seems to be less important than our need for simplicity and routine.[1]

My priority during the small amount of time I have away from my working and family life is not meeting new people but spending time alone or with trusted old friends. These three or four close friends are all childless and mostly single. We do not share the same current life

stage, but we have known one another for years and have a loving and understanding friendship—and that's what I need now more than anything else. This may be because of the life phase of parenthood or the life phase of middle age. Recently, I read an interview with a fifty-two year-old famous Hollywood actress in a gossip magazine, and she said that "the older I get, the smaller my closest circle of friends becomes." She called it "sorting out." You sort out the people around you and cut ties with the more difficult ones. Those who remain take you as you really are and vice versa. Maybe that's also the reason why I did not have the energy to get involved with other new comothers during this phase of my life. New relationships need energy, and I just did not have any left for them.

However, it was easy to informally connect with the parents we met around Vinzi's baby classes and our daycare provider. We got to know two or three parent couples that way. Sometimes, I situationally identify more with some of the fathers and their roles, and other times with the mothers and their roles. My role changes and is flexible, always with the goal of finding a good solution for Vinzi and giving him as much security and space for development as possible.

However, our befriended heterosexual couples with toddlers envy us for our partnership-based division of labour. Both of our jobs are about 80 per cent of fulltime, and we share the child care fifty-fifty. We take turns putting Vinzi to bed, dressing him, cooking for him, and playing with him. Or we do these things together. We are present in all care and friendship contexts. For the housework and house management, I do more because my disorder tolerance limit is lower than Katharina's, which leads to constant quarrels. But, nevertheless, we still hear from our friends that we share everything (meaning childcare and breadwinning). Our friends with toddlers are generally well-educated women and men who have become parents later in life after completing university and getting good jobs. But gender equality stopped exactly at the time of childbirth, even for couples past forty. The men spend even more time at work and the women work half-days, get up at night when the babies cry, and pick up the children from kindergarten.

There is a feminist backlash that feeds on the overburdening of families and capitalistic lifestyle. Most of the women around us earn less than men, and there are plenty of other social and occupational factors that make us seem even closer to a traditional gender role model than in our parents' day. At that time, there might have been more women who were housewives, but there was a clear desire for change. Women were fighting for the right and the chance to work, and men were beginning to see the benefits of being close and present with their children, and they started to demand their share of it. These values are—at least in our social and educational class—pretty much standard. But then things do not work out in line with these values because of time resources, money, career progression, caring duties, and children being born later in life. If we were a hetero couple, what would our situation be? Katharina earns more and is more invested in her career path than I am, so we resemble to a certain extent traditional gender roles with male-female couples, in which I take the women's role. But Katharina is also a full-blooded mother and would not give up her share of parenting at any cost. I also cannot imagine giving up my work, which makes me happy, is fulfilling, and secures my autonomy.

We may not be old school, second-wave feminists like those from the 1970s and 1980s. Instead, we were socialized in the 1990s, and come from the lusty, riot grrrl, and queer-transgender movements of these days. But we've already learned so much from our more or less feminist and more or less independent biological mothers and fathers. My parents stayed together and live in absolute equality. Katharina's parents are divorced, and Katharina's mother could only afford the divorce and her later good life because she always worked during her prime working years. We also learned from our social mothers—elder friends, literati, artists, theorists, and queer and feminist activists, who taught us about the social meanings and limits of gender roles and were pioneers and fighters for autonomy and gender equality. This knowledge is written in our social DNA and that influences our relationship, too. Sometimes, it helps that we are two women. We stand on certain identity grounds that make some negotiations and struggles in our relationship more egalitarian, some gender attributes less self-evident, and let some social pressures or freedoms equally affect us both. Some people wonder whether we fight about and discuss the same problems as heterosexual couples, such as housework, money, and education. Yes, of course we do. There is a systemic lack of compatibility that every family feels, but, at least there is no gender bias about these issues in our relationship.

That doesn't mean it hasn't been challenging to find a balance between us. Our own space has become pretty tight. The real problem is a lack of time. We have no parents who could look after the children; the people in question are either already dead, too old, or don't have a good relationship with my little family. Katharina's siblings also have small children; they are also a resource but not to an extent that we can leave Vinzi alone with them, at least not yet. So Katharina and I are pretty much dependent on each other if we want to have free space. We hardly have any common quality time together, unless we hire a babysitter. But most of the babysitting time is used up by the requirements of our working schedule, and little is left for candlelight dinners. But today I am finally sitting here alone in Durham, Northern England, in a coffee shop on an ancient bridge in this medieval town and have time for myself, time to write.

When Vinzi was born in 2015, this initiated a second coming-out period in my life. My first coming out in the 1990s was so long ago that I hardly remember it today. But one thing was always clear to me: It is out of the question for me to keep the important things in my life in the closet. Today, I think that this attitude shows how brave I was but also how spoiled: I lived in a country and in a family, as well as worked professional contexts, that have always allowed me to be myself without too much existential cost.

My first coming out was difficult with regards to parents and family. Professionally, however, being gay did not play a big role then. The central place in my life in the 1990s was the university, and back then it was even rather hip to be queer. I was active in the queer scene, as I wrote in magazines and organized parties and meetings. Not only was I out, I was in the middle of it; I took part in this development of queer culture in Austria and pushed it forwards.

My second coming out as a queer mom was more difficult. I now lived an adult life and worked in a sometimes professional, stiff, and formal field of work, as a management consultant with my own little company. A share of my customers currently come from the social and nonprofit sector, but a significant proportion of my work comes from the business sector. For many of those customers, being gay, out, and proud is not common.

It was inconceivable for me to justify my prolonged absence for Vinzent's birth and my parental leave with excuses and lies. If I had been a biological mother, I would not have needed any special explanation: I would have had a baby bump, everyone would have congratulated me, and nobody would have been surprised at my absence from work. As a comother, it is different. Suddenly, I sent out emails that I was going on parental leave without any previous physical sign of pregnancy. So I had to explain to my customers that I was becoming a comother, not just a mother. In this, I had the support of my business partner, Rotija, who is part of an ethnic minority in Austria—the Carinthian Slovenes. She is feminist, and as a member of a discriminated group, she is sensitive to diversity in general. Rotija knew from the beginning that Katharina and I wanted to have a child and has always been supportive, which was enormously helpful to me at this time.

Vinzent has been cared for since he was six months old by our beloved "daycare-mother," Sabine, who also looks after four other toddlers. Sabine and her family have kind of adopted our child, and they are his closest chosen-family relationship. Whenever we brought Vinzent to Sabine, we could be sure he was safe, secure, and loved. In this coming autumn, he will leave this safe place and go out into a kindergarten, a more institutional space. We visited at least thirty kindergartens in the past year, and you could, perhaps, say that our kindergarten search has become a little neurotic. (And I say that as a Viennese dyke, as, of course, Freud was raised in Vienna, and Katharina, as a child, lived on Berggasse 25, where Freud himself used to live, in number twenty-nine.) Most of the time, I finished the kindergarten appointment with something like: "We're a rainbow family. This means that Vinzi has two mothers. I am the comother. Do you have any experience with such a family or would you like to know something about it?" They would often say, "That's no problem for us at all. We are quite open to that!" Only two kindergarten principals wanted to know something more and invited us to a team meeting.

Starting next fall, Vinzent will go to a kindergarten with twenty-four other children. I'm not sure how it happened, but it's a Catholic kindergarten. Vinzi's best friend will also go there. It was a gut decision; we are somehow confident that this will be a good, bourgeois nursery for Vinzi, as his complex and turbulent world, and that we will find other parents in the nursery with whom we can coexist easily or even become friends. There is also the hope that we can finally befriend parents with whom we can share childcare a little. Going to a Catholic kindergarten as queer mothers is a bit absurd, ambivalent, and contradictory, but that's the way our life has been lately. The Catholic kindergarten has assured us that they are quite open to our family form and that families have become so diverse these days that for the children it's all quite normal and self-evident. But what we really liked was the statement of the head of staff: "Please give us some time to learn!"

In this kindergarten, the majority of children speak German well or at passable level—either as a first language or as a well-established second language. This is in contrast to many public kindergartens in Vienna, especially Ottakring, our beloved migrants' district, where we have lived and worked for the past ten years and where the share of children who are migrants in the kindergartens is very high. We are not xenophobic or racist—at least I believe so. I'm not sure if this is still true and valid because when it comes to the educational and development perspectives of our child, our desire for diversity suddenly came under pressure, which is a difficult confession to make.

They say that a child will ground you. This saying is correct. Many of my ideas and ideals have been made concrete by the existence of Vinzi, in the best sense as well as in a disillusioning one. There is such great love and responsibility attached to this wonderful child that we decide nothing recklessly or merely in principle. When I was younger, I was much more experimental with regard to my social and relationship life than I am now; I was in open, polyamorous relationships and was interested in communes and alternative cohabitation projects. I eventually gave up the explicitly polyamorous life due to being overburdened both emotionally and pragmatically. Now with the birth of Vinzi, polyamory has once again snuck into my life as an (almost) normal nuclear family triad. Katharina and I very much wanted to find a biological father from our circle of male friends who could have played a more active role in our lives. We searched a long time, but unfortunately it did not work out. Vinzi was conceived with the help of an open sperm donation and an insemination in a Danish sperm donation clinic. Vinzi has basic information about his biological father and his family background; he will be able to contact him later if he wishes. Whether our sperm donor wants to maintain contact with Vinzi later, and if so to what extent, we do not know.

In a month, I'll be fifty. In terms of a possible one hundred year lifespan, I have arrived to mid-life. But, honestly, how many people reach one hundred years, and who really wants to become that old? So, if I'm comparing myself to my parents and grandparents, then there's at best a third of lifetime ahead of me, and I hope to be able to accompany Vinzi's life until he's in his thirties. I studied philosophy, and when I was younger, I wanted to immigrate to France; I saw myself as an ideal descendant of the decadent French women of the 1920s and 1960s. In my spiritual heart, I also regarded myself as a little bit of a 1968 hippie, especially since that is the year of my birth. And I still believe that my life would also be full of meaning and fulfillment without children. In any case, love has always been the central element of my life. I have loved men and women and sometimes at the same time. But I have never thought so much of children or wished to have any, even if they were included in my general philanthropy. I simply could not imagine how so small a person could fulfill and enrich life so much. But thanks to Katharina, I became a parent and I can say that my child has become one of the great loves in my life and now gives me the greatest joie de vivre.

Postscript

During the writing of this article I learned that in English comother or coparenting has a different meaning than it has in the similar German term. In German, it is commonly used for the nonbiological mother in a lesbian women couple. I learned that in English, coparenting means parenting between two partners who are now no longer together or, sometimes, how the parenting relationship works between two or more parents. Therefore, I was asked by Sherri[2] why I call myself a comother rather than a mother. She asked me what the term "comother" helps me understand or express about my experience of parenting.

I think there is no logical answer; it's about the process and the struggle of queer parenting and developing identity of queer and social parenthood. Identity is always connected with names, and queer identity is also about fluxes in names and identities: therefore, I am Nadja, I am Mami, and I am a mother. I was also suggested to be Mapa (the words "mother" and "father" combined in an artificial new word), but I didn't respond to this title. I'm a mother; I am the mother—I am the comother. My brother even suggested that I should be called "father" or take the father role. In most respects, I call and regard myself today as a mother and a normal mother. But if it were already normal to everybody, there would not be a need for the present collection of stories and there would not be a need to exclude heterosexual or biological parents. We all (together) would just report about the experiences with our children and families. But we and society, and our co-parents, and our families and friends, and kindergartens and schools make a difference; therefore, we make it, too. This is the interactional dynamics of identity, but it is not fixed; it is moving on towards new ways of being and fulfilling roles. Maybe I could ignore or overlook the difference and perform just being normal; in this case, there would be no need to write about my parenthood here. Most of the time, I actually do ignore the difference, and today— more than two years after I started the article—I regard myself much more normal or, rather, I have more self-understanding than in the beginning. This is the work: reflecting upon your identity over history and through the necessary process of becoming. And what will be the result? The result, I hope, is being special—to me, my son, my beloved— and being normal to the same people and to some others, as well.

Endnotes

1. Two years later, I checked in with a coparent group there, which was a good experience.
2. Sherri Martin-Baron, the co-editor of this book collection.

Chapter Eight

Making a Mama Bear

Melissa Boyce

There's a four-year-old girl who sleeps in the bedroom across the hall. Her olive skin and deep brown eyes resemble an old photo of me from when I was about her age. From the dimples that form on either side of her lips when she grins to her straight, brown hair, she cannot be mistaken for anyone else's daughter but mine.

I remember dreaming of her while planning my adult life when I was a teenager. I even had her name picked out: Stevie, like the queen of rock herself. I was going to have a daughter just like me—a tomboy perhaps, athletic and strong, maybe a little outspoken at times—but more than anything, she would have a fighter's heart like her mama.

In my planning, I knew I would need to find someone who I could trust with starting a family—someone who was responsible and who could perhaps help me to become responsible too. Sure, I had dated here and there and even had a couple of long-term relationships, but it never felt like the right time, and, in retrospect, it was never the right person.

As recent as even seven years ago, I would not have dreamed I would be a mom today. I could barely take care of myself. My portion of the fridge that I shared with my roommate was always bare. Fast-food wrappers adorned the side console of my beige SUV, which was almost always on empty. I worked a retail job that barely paid the bills, and, sometimes, it didn't at all. It wasn't for my lack of working plenty of hours at the store but for my lack of responsibility. Who wants to pay for groceries or gas when you can eat a quick bite out and drink beer with friends? No muss, no fuss. I was a child, and I didn't have room in my life for one of my own. Shortly after my twenty-ninth birthday, though, I met the love of my life. Erin came into my life during a time when I was unsure of what I wanted. She happened to be what I needed, too.

It was a love affair like I had never had before. Up until Erin, I had only dated men. That plan that I had put together so many years before never included another woman. I had always imagined I would raise a child with a man, but as they say, everything happens for a reason. Perhaps the reason I never found someone to make a family with before was because I needed to find my true self in the journey—the journey that led me to her.

After nearly a year of dating—which included moving in together, my changing jobs, and a few months of family strife—we took our relationship to the next level. We had a few small discussions here and there regarding starting a family. It was strange that it wasn't strange at all for us to talk about it so freely and openly. Of course, that just made us both agree even more that we were, in fact, ready to start a family, just not any time soon.

The catch here was that Erin would have to be the one to carry our child for us. I had spent years in and out of doctor's offices, taking tests, and trying new drugs to sustain any hope of my bearing a child. This was all a result of being diagnosed with endometriosis. What a life for a woman in her twenties, right?

Since I had already come to terms with not being able to carry a child of my own, I had convinced myself that I didn't want a family by the time Erin came around, even though there was still a sliver of desire to have children I had pushed way, way back into the dark corners of my brain. Although that desire resurfaced once Erin was in my life and we were starting to have those serious life-changing discussions, it wasn't meant to be immediately life changing. We were planners, and we wanted this for our future, but not so soon that a plan couldn't be in place—that is until one afternoon. During a routine annual visit to my gynecologist, my inability to have children took an immediate halt and did an about face. The biggest change in my personal desires and goals came quickly and without warning.

Lying on the table, both feet in the air with the aid of stirrups, I shockingly received the news from the latest in the lineup of doctors to take on my case that not only was I ready to start trying for a baby, but I was actually encouraged to do so. Apparently, the birth control with the added progesterone and the progesterone shots I had taken regularly had worked to increase the strength of my uterus and thicken its lining.

It was in that moment my doctor aggressively suggested that I start a family ASAP. Simultaneously, in that moment I knew I would have to sit Erin down and have a heavy conversation.

That night while we lay in bed talking with the blackness all around, as we did every night, I brought up the topic with hesitation. My lips quivered, and I could barely choke the sentence through my lips: "My doctor suggests I have a baby ASAP."

That was the sentence that started it all: our family planning and looking towards the now-near future. If we were going to be in it for the long haul, then there was no room for uncertainty in that mutual decision. We couldn't afford to be flippant. This was much too large, and the weight of it could collapse our relationship if we didn't make a well-thought-out plan going forwards. We're planners, remember? After many discussions, she was all in.

Our decision came with a slew of questions. How would we obtain the sperm necessary to conceive? Do we go to a donor bank or ask someone we know? Who do we know who would offer up his sperm without making our relationship complicated? Where would we find the resources and equipment necessary for donations? If I get pregnant, does that mean Erin carries our second child? Are we already thinking about a second child? It got real. Fast.

After taking a couple of weeks to gather the necessary information, and talking through many "what-ifs," it was set: We would both try to get pregnant at the same time. Yes, you read that right—at the same time!

We pushed through any qualms we might have had, and we began the preparation for conceiving a child or, in this case, children. Even before trying to find a donor, we immediately changed our diet and became more aware of what we were putting into our bodies. We promptly started a prenatal vitamin regimen, and it all felt natural and easy up to that point.

We took to the Internet to do research on where to begin. Our decision to use a donor site instead of someone we knew came as easily as the initial preparation of our bodies, and after weeks of sorting through donors online, we settled on one from our hometown. Our initial meeting was at a restaurant for lunch after having exchanged messages on the donor website for a short time. It was like online dating for our uteruses.

Our personalities matched well, and he understood the process having donated once before to a lesbian couple a few years earlier. He had a wife, three daughters, and two sons. I knew he was, at the very least, the most fertile man we could have chosen.

We settled on the technique we would all be comfortable trying. The donation would be done in a plastic medicine syringe behind a closed door and handed off to the partner not being inseminated while the targeted uterus would be ready for receiving, underneath the cloak of a bedsheet, with a speculum in place. It was the most unromantic way of creating a life, but it was the best shot we had given our circumstances.

We began this new venture in the late summer of 2014. It was everything I had not imagined about conceiving a child, but it didn't matter how intrusive or technical it was because all that I cared about was doing this with Erin. So what if we both got pregnant at the same time. More babies to love, I suppose.

We would get our hopes up each month, having timed everything to a tee, but each month would result in no pregnancy for either of us. Countless tears flowed from my eyes but always behind closed doors; I never let Erin see. I began realizing after each test was taken just how much I really wanted this for us. The more negative results I saw, the more desperate I became internally.

After a total of five months of trying, I had all but given up. I had watched the last three months go by with no blue lines on my ovulation strips. Erin's ovulation tests were the same solid line every single month. If either of us was going to get pregnant, it was going to be her. I knew it.

I began to become jealous of her always-positive readings and the more I timed everything biologically, the more disappointed I felt seeing my own vacant strip. I tried tricking myself into changing my way of thinking. After all, I had done it before with convincing myself that I was okay not having kids before Erin. So, this shouldn't be too hard to do.

I remember one night in particular. I looked at Erin sitting across the dinner table from me and said a silent wish to myself: "If a baby is in our future, please let Erin be the first of us to get pregnant. She wants this so badly. I do too, but I really want her to have this."

On the evening of January 20, 2015, I received a phone call from Erin while I was at work. "I just took a test and it came out positive!" she said. Admittedly, I could feel the gut-wrenching hue of green wash over me, and my tears were of both happiness and jealousy.

I raced home, and we embraced. She took another test the next morning just to be sure, and the positive sign on the strip confirmed our results from the night before. A new chapter in our lives was about to begin, and, thankfully, we had each other to experience it all.

Once the dust settled and the big picture became a bit clearer to us both, we discussed our options and whether going forwards with our attempts to inseminate me was a good idea or not. We landed on a mutual decision, and I informed our donor that due to Erin's pregnancy, and the added stress of it all, we would postpone my attempts for a later date. As expected, he generously offered his time and donation for any date we wished, whenever we were ready to try again.

As the pages on my calendar flipped and the months passed by, more and more of a buildup began to form inside me. I didn't know what it was at the time. It felt heavy, a type of grit weighing me down, but I hadn't the faintest idea what this feeling was that was taking over me.

As with any kind of buildup, it reached the brim and then spilled over. I realized exactly what the feeling was one day as we were leaving the doctor's office for a prenatal checkup. It happened to be the same doctor's visit that revealed the sex of the baby. I was torn between being ecstatic that we were having a girl and being blatantly jealous that I was not the one carrying her.

I hid my emotions for several reasons, but mostly because I didn't want that happy moment to be clouded with my own resentment. That was it. That was the feeling I had been developing inside myself: resentment.

We already had names picked out for either sex, so when we got home that day I chose to embrace the joy over the indignation, and with our newfound knowledge, I created a banner to post on social media so we could announce to our cyberworld that we were expecting a girl: Miss Stevie Lee. The envy I felt ebbed and flowed from feeling painful desire to being a grateful partner and back again more times than I can count. One thing I kept reminding myself was that Stevie, the baby girl I used to dream about, was still going to be part of me somehow. I was still going to be one of the most important persons in her life, and knowing this brought me peace.

As I mentioned earlier, Stevie was always going to be my daughter's name. Erin liked it, too, and we went with it. Lee is Erin's mother's name—a nod to the hardworking woman who raised Erin to be the selfless person she is today—so I was most definitely on board with that homage. The next child in our little family could have my mom's name as her middle name, or my dad's name should the baby I carry be a boy, and we would be able to honour them as well. It was our plan. I liked it. I felt more included with this plan and going forwards in the next few months; it helped to mitigate any negative emotions I might have had about the whole thing.

The second trimester for Erin was a fun one. Well, maybe I'm imagining it to be more fun than it actually was, since I was on the outside looking in. Pregnancy brain hit her hard, and I laughed every time she misplaced an object or cried over a nonsentimental TV commercial. She warned me every time: "I'm going to make fun of you even more when you go through this."

At the very least, I could prepare myself for the torment of emotional peaks and valleys. I had a good while before we would even consider getting me pregnant. Erin was still three months out, and we weren't planning to start trying again until the baby was at least six months old.

Every two weeks, from the first time we announced Erin's pregnancy, Erin would post photos of her growing belly on her social media, and so many of our family and friends would comment or throw us a "like." It was nice. I knew my time would come to be able to show off my own pregnancy photos as well. I held onto that notion.

Occasionally, someone would privately text me asking how Erin was doing, or a coworker would sometimes ask me questions about the pregnancy. It was nice of them to inquire, but there were so many times I wanted to just tell them to contact her themselves rather than ask me. I felt like the middle man. Just when I was getting myself used to being the outsider in the pregnancy, people would magnify the fact that I was not the one who was pregnant.

The questions came furiously. How's the pregnancy going? Does she crave any outrageous foods? Does she make you do what I used to make my husband do, like rub my swollen feet or drive me around town just to get the right kind of ice cream? If she's the one pregnant, does that make you the dad? Who gets to celebrate Mother's Day? Or will you share it? Why don't you just take Father's Day, since you're not really the baby's mother?

That last one killed me. It was the dagger that pierced my heart and caused so much of the resentment and frustration inside me to change from envy to pure, unadulterated, red-hot heat. How could anyone consider me less than a mother just because I didn't carry the child? The question came from someone who had randomly texted me after not speaking to each other for years because we had dated years prior, but I felt no need for his friendship.

After putting him in his place and letting him know just how involved I had been up to that point (of course not going into detail) and that I am Stevie's mother too, he took the conversation up a notch. Here I thought I had squashed any chance of the conversation escalating. Boy was I wrong! He brought religion into the conversation and demanded I understand his stance that every child needs a father and a mother. He insisted that any child brought into a home with same-sex parents would be tarnished and would further tarnish society. He told me that my lifestyle was not just a sin but just plain wrong. He turned from aggressively denying my role as a mother to downright casting shame on me for believing that two women could possibly have sexual relations in the first place. Only through sexual relations can you create life, and if two men can't make a baby and two women can't make a baby, then it isn't sex. Not real sex.

I was beyond heated. My reply took several minutes to type out via text, but the anger that built up inside me poured out through my fingertips and I was on a roll. I can spare you from what I actually said, as I'm sure you didn't begin reading this chapter believing you would read such vulgarity. Rest assured—I gave him what for.

Looking back on it now, I am actually grateful for that interaction. It's the moment I can pinpoint where I began feeling like a proud mama bear, ready to protect her cub. It was that same moment when I let go of all of my resentment towards the situation and, really, towards Erin. I still can't believe that this text exchange was what flipped the script for me, but regardless of the circumstances, I am glad it happened.

Erin didn't even know I had those feelings until recently. I never let on because I didn't want her to feel hated. I didn't hate her. In all the time we've been together, I have never felt an ounce of hatred towards her. I only wanted to spare her my woe-is-me rants, and in doing so, I bottled it up. It might have come out in a rant towards her instead of that stupid, ignorant man from my past. I'm glad I chose to spew my wrath on the deserving party. It helped clear a new path for me, one filled with celebration and joy. I chose to view that exchange as a cathartic release, and then I simply took control of my feelings, one moment at a time.

One month shy of Stevie's due date, we were given two separate baby showers. Luckily, each shower was a celebration of life and love, and our family and friends celebrated us both. They showered us together and congratulated both of us instead of just doting on Erin. Sure, there were lovely comments about her pregnancy glow, and I appreciated those just as much as she, but for the most part, I felt included, finally.

Erin's due date, October 1, came quicker than I had imagined. One o'clock in the morning the contractions started. I pushed back all of my nerves and put on the brave mama bear mask. I watched Erin struggle through the pain of contractions and through nausea from the pain meds; I wiped vomit from her face twice, as her body reacted to the nauseating pain relievers. Thirteen long hours later, we welcomed the loudest crier in the hospital: Stevie Lee. Yep. She's loud, just like her Mama M, and right on time, just like her Mama E.

Erin was so damn strong and patient throughout it all, and I was so grateful for what she had just done for our family. I felt no resentment, only gratitude. Erin's strength was challenged immediately after I cut the umbilical cord. A nurse walked Stevie over to get cleaned up while the doctor stitched Erin. Just as the doctor stood up from her stool, blood began rushing out of the stitches and onto the bed. After several minutes and numerous gauzes put in place to stop the bleeding, Erin, lethargic from having just given birth, was back to a safe position and able to hold our baby girl. In those several minutes, watching the doctor sew her up and seeing all the blood she lost, I panicked but never let it show.

In the following three months, we felt so lucky to have such a calm baby in Stevie, who slept through the night beginning at week six, that our decision to wait six months postdelivery to inseminate me for baby number two was an easy one to forget. We contacted our donor to start as soon as possible and agreed to wait a couple months so I could get my body prepped again: prenatal vitamins, eating better, no more alcohol—all the same things as before.

I scheduled a doctor's visit at the same women's clinic that Erin attended for all of her prenatal checkups. I liked the facility and the faculty; best yet, they already knew me because I hadn't missed one appointment with Erin throughout her pregnancy. Our new plan was underway.

But as with previous objectives I've made in my life, this, too, was thwarted right as we closed in on a starting date to inseminate me again.

It was a visit to a doctor once again that steered me towards yet another direction in life. This time it was PCOS (polycystic ovarian syndrome). That's an acronym I had never heard before and one I wish I never had to learn.

My doctor informed me that she was weary at my last visit and had my blood work sent in to determine my hormone levels. Sure enough, all signs pointed to PCOS. What does this mean? It means my body hates me! No, actually, it means my body creates more male hormones than usual, resulting in enlarged ovaries and small clusters of cysts throughout. It also causes weight gain, abnormal hair growth, irregular and painful periods, as well as infertility, which was another word I didn't like to hear.

My doctor reassured me that many women with PCOS change their diet and exercise regimens and go on having multiple babies. There wasn't a need to worry just yet. Whew! She insisted I undergo some more bloodwork as well as have an ultrasound done to be sure this was the case. The tests were scheduled strategically during a time when I was supposed to be ovulating. I was told it is easier to get results that way.

Weeks later, after waiting impatiently for the results, I sat in the same office where the doctor had broken the news to me about my possibly having PCOS. Results from the second batch of blood work confirmed our fears. I definitely had it. The results also indicated no ovulation. Worse yet, the ultrasound pointed to a crooked uterus. Great, I had spent all those years being straight! Was this a parallel to my new sex life? (I'm joking. It's easier to joke in retrospect. Trust me.)

The full diagnosis I was given that day was "PCOS with ovulatory dysfunction." In short, bearing any children of my own was not going to happen. Even if I controlled the symptoms of PCOS and maintained balanced hormone levels, I did not produce the eggs to fertilize. All efforts to inseminate me would be for naught. I was relieved to have answers, but I was absolutely devastated with the results.

This all meant my having another important talk with Erin. We were getting good at important talks as luck would have it. As I explained to her what my body was going through and what it wasn't allowing me to do, Erin hugged me and we embraced for a long while. I texted our donor shortly after and explained the situation. He wished us well with Stevie and encouraged me to focus on her and embrace all the good things that she has already brought to my life. It was a nice sentiment during that hard time. I obviously appreciate that man for many things, but his compassion precedes them all.

I was determined not to let this new roadblock convince me that jealousy was the route to take. There are times, even today, that I look at Erin and envy her. She got to carry our daughter and feel her kick from the depths of her womb. She got to hold her for the very first time. She got to breastfeed her and stay home with her for three whole months, which overshadowed my one-month leave of absence from work. After the scare following the delivery, and because of the horrible impact the pregnancy had on Erin's body overall, causing back pain and a shift in her pelvis, we had already agreed that she would not carry another child for us. So this meant that now there would be no possibility of honouring my side of the family with a namesake.

Erin would always be tied to Stevie. It wasn't a bond I could have with our daughter, nor would I be able to experience it for myself with any of the children we had wanted to include in our family in the future. These were all things I knew I would have to come to terms with, and while it did take some time, I did just that.

It's been four years since we received the news that I could not give birth to a child. Stevie is now four, and if you looked at her or had a conversation with her, I'm convinced you would know in your heart that she is my daughter. I might not have carried her in my womb, but since the moment Erin and I saw that little blue line, I have carried her in my heart.

I won't say that being jealous is a distant feeling from me now. Sometimes jealousy creeps its way back, ready to strike and sink its fangs into me, but I avoid it swiftly and recount all of the ways she is mine. Jealousy is an ugly look on me, but I'm doing my best to wash it away daily. Instead, when the feeling dissipates, and it always does, I am free to rejoice in the love that fills our home.

It helps that our daughter somehow looks just like me. It's a small victory for us nonbiological moms, but I'll take it!

Chapter Nine

From Ambivalence to All In: Biology Does Not Matter, Love Is All That Counts!

Raechel Johns

I can't remember where we were at the time, but I can remember that sinking feeling when my partner told me early in our relationship that she wanted to be a mum. I had not planned to have children, and her revelation that she wanted to be a mum surely marked the end of our promising, new relationship. Yet as I drove away from her at the end of our date, I felt an increasing sense of excitement, too. I was ambivalent about parenting yet strangely excited by the idea, too. I didn't understand where to go from here. What if I signed up to a lifetime as a parent simply because it was what she wanted? I knew I had to think this over. It would be one of the most serious decisions I would ever make.

I asked her to give me time. I asked for us to have three months, during which time our relationship would proceed, or not, without discussions of the future. True to her word, she didn't talk about children. Her self-control was remarkable, given she must have been wondering where we'd end up. I guess she had faith that whatever would be would be. Her intentions were certainly clear, though; mine were grey.

Growing up, I had a moment where I had wanted to be a parent, but I hadn't wanted to be a mother. I distinctly remember thinking, "I would have kids if I could be a dad." Perhaps, it was a sexist or stereotypical view, but it was my view, nevertheless. Being a secondary parent was appealing, but I didn't want to give up my career goals to have a child, and I didn't know if I could do it all. I'd grown up with a stay-at-home mum, and although I knew plenty of career women who made it work, I wasn't sure if I wanted to make it work. I didn't have that strong maternal drive. Besides, I couldn't be a dad, so I'd put all thoughts of children aside. I commenced my career and fell deeply in love with the work that I did. I wasn't missing anything in my life; I wasn't feeling sad or frustrated by this decision. It wasn't really even a decision, merely a fleeting thought in my childhood. There was no real sense of longing for children, even though I'd always liked children. I decided I'd be the fabulous aunty, and I adored my nieces and nephews, and that was enough. My friends started having children, and I never once waivered on my decision. I was childfree by choice.

But then I met her and she wanted kids. Somehow, this made me think. Now that I'd come out and everything made sense, could I be a parent, after all, with another mum by my side? Because same-sex couples redefined relationships, could we redefine family? Could that change the way I saw parenting? I knew I loved children, although I wasn't particularly a baby person. I was fascinated by childhood development, and I knew that together, we could do it.

During my time of thinking, I read books. I didn't even know what type of parent I wanted to be; I didn't even know how to become a parent. I needed to read parenting theory. I needed stories about same-sex couples raising kids. I needed to learn about child development. I needed stories from kids raised by queer parents. And I needed to know whether the turkey baster really was a thing. It wasn't that I was naïve; it was simply that the thought had never crossed my mind. But in reading these books and pondering these questions, I decided I did want to parent, but my children did not need to be biologically connected to me. In fact, given my partner and I couldn't possibly conceive a biological mix of the two of us, I pondered whether our children needed to be biologically connected to either of us or whether we could give a home to kids in need of a stable home.

I asked my partner how many children she wanted, and she said that as long as she had one, she'd be happy. Having very close bonds to my sisters, I felt differently. I decided that if I were going to take the plunge and completely change my life, I would have at least three children. My partner was happy to agree, so we chatted about different ways to become parents. We went to a fostering information evening, we rang the government adoption folk, and we discussed ways to get one of us pregnant. We signed up for a foster-care information session. That evening, I had it all worked out. I decided we should adopt one child and birth one each. My partner simply nodded along. We had no idea what the future would hold, and she's much less of a planner than I am. We did agree, however, without question that she would be a stay-a-home mum, and I could continue my career. "Are you happy to give up your career?" I asked her, a little worried.

"I get my dream," she'd said, happily. We both got what we wanted that way. It seemed to be an ideal fit for us!

We signed up for foster-care training at the same time as we started trying for a baby. What would be would be. We assumed, incorrectly, that achieving a pregnancy would be faster than training, getting assessed, and getting a permanent placement, but we weren't sure. We completed our training and our assessment, and within six months, we graduated, went on a holiday overseas, and returned home to a phone call that we needed to sign some paperwork urgently. The staff member came rushing to our house on a Sunday evening to get the document signed, which surprised us, and by the Tuesday, we received a phone call offering us a four-month-old baby boy. We jumped at the chance, and I encouraged my partner to quit her job. She was reluctant and was justified in her reluctance when, the next day, we were told the baby had had a family member step forwards. "It could be ages until the next call," my partner said, but I disagreed. Either way, I thought it made sense for her to enjoy some time at home. She didn't resign, and three long days passed with no phone call. It felt like it might never happen. We were so impatient by then, and in some strange way, we briefly grieved the baby we'd never even met.

On the Friday, however, I'd left my office and gone to a conference room to do some writing. I did this every two weeks with my academic colleagues to have a mini writing retreat, but on this particular day, no one else turned up. I was lost in my thoughts, tapping away at my computer and listening to music, when my phone rang. The agency wondered if we would be interested in becoming carers for a sibling group. "It's very likely they'd be with you forever, but no guarantees just yet," the case worker told me. The words repeated in my head, over and over. I rang my partner who was just leaving work for the day. "Meet you at home?" she said. I hurriedly packed up my computer and work for the weekend, shaking, and rushed out the door. We spent that afternoon discussing it, sitting on the couch. We had thought we'd adopt one child, and here we were discussing a potential sibling group. I thought my partner would be the one to say "no," but suddenly she said, "We did this to grow our family, and this grows our family. These kids need a home. Let's do it." I was shocked, and I immediately rang the caseworker back. "Think about it over the weekend," she said to me. "We'll chat again Monday." "But we know now we want to do this," I responded. I wanted it locked in; I didn't want to spend the weekend going back and forth. I didn't want us to change our minds. "Yes, that's great, but let's just leave it til Monday, and then we can discuss it again." She didn't want us rushing into the biggest decision of our lives.

On the Monday, I rang her first thing, and we started to make arrangements to meet the children. My partner gave her notice to finish work, but I also talked to my boss about taking a few weeks off so my partner could work her notice period. I ended up staying at home with the children for the first few weeks. "I'm getting experience as the stay-at-home mum," I said to her. "So that I will know what you're going through!"

After we'd had the children just two weeks, we went to a rainbow family playgroup. I loved meeting all the families and suddenly feeling a part of the "gayby boom." We had something in common with all the other parents—having children, if nothing else. One woman in the group was about six-months pregnant, and as the discussion turned to pregnancy and birth, everyone exchanged their stories. The group turned to us; we had remained silent. We had no pregnancy or birth stories to share, and we finally confessed this to the group. Just as quickly as I'd felt part of things, I suddenly felt like we didn't belong—that somehow the experiences of pregnancy and birth that we'd lacked meant we didn't actually belong among this group of parents. Real parents.

The group itself was welcoming, and they were surprised to hear that we'd only had the children such a short time. "They look so settled with you," the people exclaimed repeatedly. "You're absolutely their parents!" Yet on the way home, I said to my partner that I felt we didn't really fit in. We weren't yet legitimately parents, but we were doing everything that parents do. We didn't return for some time. We didn't return again until we felt like legitimate parents, when we felt we'd earned the right to be there, which doesn't come as quickly as it does when you birth a baby.

"Maybe we should go to a foster care playgroup," I said, when chatting to our caseworker about it all. "Do they have those?" She shook her head and explained that it's better for these children to not socialize only with foster children—a fact that makes total sense in hindsight.

Over time, we began to feel like parents. We enrolled them in preschools; we decorated their bedrooms, and we were who they ran to whenever they were upset. Suddenly, they began calling my partner "Mum." Our eldest child turned to her one day and said, "You're my Mum," and my partner felt so proud. The other kids quickly followed. I'd never wanted to be called "Mum," so there was no sense of competition, and I was truly delighted for her. It was really important to us, too, that it had evolved so naturally. Finally, we got the much-awaited news that they were staying with us forever. I gradually started encouraging them to call me "Mama." I'd not been bothered at all that they'd called me by my name, but I felt like a babysitter when I picked my son up from preschool and he called me by my first name and asked where Mum was. I was anxious about what the other parents must think. I suppose that my desire to be called Mama was, therefore, based on other parents around me rather than my relationship with the children. I knew I was Mama by this point and never particularly felt I needed to have a Mum or Mama title to be their parent.

During all of this time with our children, we were trying to conceive, rather unsuccessfully, with the intention that I would carry.

At the commencement of our conception journey, we had invited friends over for dinner—a couple we were friends with—with the intention of asking one of them to be our sperm donor. As I fussed, cleaned, and cooked a three-course meal, I was reminded of the first time my partner had visited my house, and I'd fussed and cleaned for her. I felt like we were wining and dining our friends, and it had parallels to a first date. The butterflies in my stomach certainly made me feel that way. Our dinner felt strangely formal, even though we'd hung out with these guys many times, casually. Finally, we asked one to be our donor, and his partner for permission around this. "I was waiting for this question," our friend admitted, and he said would be more than thrilled to be our donor. After a cycle of testing for both him and me, we commenced the process. We used ovulation monitors, and he would visit a few times a month. He would knock on the bedroom door with the sperm and leave the house to give us our privacy. We would insert the sperm through a needleless syringe, as our hands shook, and we laughed heaps. Each month, we would test and shrug our shoulders, making plans for the next cycle. I set myself a challenge for each cycle—I'd plan a thick book to read, a new recipe book to follow, a new TV series to watch, restaurants to try, or an exercise program to do. I started a new dance class; I caught up with friends. I planned weekends away, and we took the children away, swam in the hotel pool, and dined out. Each and every cycle I set myself a different task or activity to look forwards to—to help me take my mind off things to get through the two-week wait and the inevitable disappointment. After eighteen months of repeated cycles, with our donor on call, we finally agreed this wasn't working, and we would need to go down the clinic route. We didn't want our friend to have to go through this, so we had a teary meeting and told him our plans.

We excitedly commenced looking at American donor profiles, and I tried to find one that resembled my partner in both looks and personality. At some point, I remember laughing and exclaiming, "I don't think introverts donate sperm! They're all extroverts!" Yet we finally found a donor that resembled her—the eyes, the hobbies, and the way he described himself. He seemed perfect, but the disappointment wasn't over. Before we had even started our first cycle, we were contacted by the clinic. Australian customs withheld the sperm for inspection, and it had died in transit. We could only laugh, and the clinic dispatched more, free of charge.

The disappointment kept following. We did five medicated IUI cycles before agreeing with the doctor that we needed to move to IVF. I was apprehensive about taking this step. It seemed to be such a gruelling process from what we'd heard. But thankfully IVF was pretty easy on me, until I got pregnant. The first cycle worked, but I'd overresponded, and after finding out I was pregnant, I landed in hospital with severe ovarian hyperstimulation. I was hospitalized for over a week, and they drained my stomach of over ten litres of fluid and put me on drips and transfusions. That was an awful start to a fairly awful pregnancy, but at the end of my hospital stay, they put me in a wheelchair and wheeled me down to the doctor's office to scan the baby, my partner walking along beside me. The baby was only five weeks along by this point, so there wasn't much to see, but the sac brought tears to our eyes anyway. The doctor assured us that the sicker I was, the healthier the baby would be.

"This is going to be one healthy baby," I often said to my partner during the pregnancy.

My partner and I suffered through the pregnancy, and many times I felt envious of friends and people in online groups who were enjoying their first pregnancy without children to look after. Because my pregnancy was so physically challenging and we had young children that needed physical support—getting them dressed, bathing and feeding them, putting them into car seats, changing nappies—I regularly thought that we'd done it the wrong way around. I thought we should have had a birth baby before our permanent placement, but I quickly snapped myself out of that thought. We had left the whole thing up to a strange combination of fate and science, and it had clearly worked out the way it was meant to be, despite the hardships I faced. My partner tried to offer support but couldn't relate to the physical hardships I was going through. I had severe morning sickness, carpal tunnel syndrome, preeclampsia, and so many other pregnancy challenges. It was all so overwhelming, and the women in my partner's family had had textbook pregnancies, so I could appreciate her difficulty in knowing how to support me.

During the pregnancy, I noticed that the attention about the unborn baby was focused on me, almost 100 per cent. I tried to change it. I would talk about how excited my partner was, how she had been busy preparing, and how the children were excitedly anticipating a new sibling. That the focus was on me as a mother was a little unnerving, as it was a role that still didn't feel completely natural to me. I needed people to not celebrate the pregnancy so much and, instead, celebrate us as parents, together. But I also knew that once the baby was here, and my partner was taking the primary caretaker role, the roles would be reversed, so I tried to not worry too much.

I ended up having an emergency C-section when it was evident that the baby wasn't doing well, due to the preeclampsia. About ten doctors, nurses, and midwives appeared in my hospital room, out of the blue, and hurriedly prepared me for surgery. I was alarmed. "My partner is at home," I said. "We're not going without her." I wasn't going to birth a baby without its other parent present. "We can't wait," the doctor said, apologetically but matter-of-factly—"She can meet you up there if she makes it, but we're going. We need this baby out now."

My cousin and mother were visiting me at the hospital and were just as alarmed, "She's having an emergency C-section," my cousin cried down the phone to my partner. "You need to come up now!" "I need to find a babysitter," my partner responded. My cousin told the room, and the doctor called out, "Bring the kids up here if she has to. We have no time to wait. We're going now."

As they wheeled me off, I realized the seriousness of this situation and screamed out my intentions. "Should I be unable to make any decisions for this baby, my partner is the other parent. She can make any decisions for the baby, and she should stay with the baby whenever possible." As I said that, tears rolled down my mother's cheeks, and, later, she asked me if I had thought I was dying. I explained I didn't once think I was dying, but as a same-sex parent family, I wanted to be clear about our intentions. In Australia, both parents can automatically go on the birth certificate—no need for second-parent adoption—but because she wasn't a biological parent, I wasn't sure if my partner would be acknowledged as parent before I'd signed all the paperwork after the birth. If I wasn't able to sign off, what would happen then? This seemed particularly important to me in the emergency situation, especially since my partner wasn't physically with me at the time.

The midwife who had been my support through the entire pregnancy assured me: "I know that you've done this together. You've been together the whole way through, so don't panic." I nodded, gratefully. Thankfully everything went smoothly from there. My partner organized a babysitter (her mother) faster than we ever had and made it up to the hospital just in time by parking in a no-parking area. Luckily, the baby was born healthy, and I recovered fairly quickly from the C-section.

My love for our baby was instant, just the way it is described, while my love for my other children had taken time to develop. My other kids were my kids, but they'd arrived as children, albeit very young ones. It took time to get to know them, and as I did, I fell in love with them. I can still remember falling in love with them. The love wasn't different; it just wasn't instant. Somehow, it's instant when a baby is born. Is that a newborn thing, or was it simply we had planned for and pictured this child for so long? Here was a connection to a kid that we'd planned, imagined, and thought about every day for eight months (my pregnancy was cut a month short), which resulted in instant love. It was a different form of preparation and imagination from the human beings that arrived on our doorstep with little notice and already established personalities.

But I knew it wasn't biology because my partner was instantly in love with the baby I birthed, too. In fact, my partner loved the baby before I did. During my pregnancy, she would say, "I love this baby already," and I would ponder how it was possible to love someone we knew absolutely nothing about. I didn't get it, and I didn't particularly feel it. Of course, I was scared of anything happening to the baby, but I felt that I didn't feel love at the time. In Australia, we use the term "clucky" to describe that need for a baby, the desire, the broodiness. Many women express their cluckiness, but I'd never experienced it. My partner had been clucky. Could that be the difference? Either way, that love certainly did arrive. It arrived for me the moment he was born, along with many other emotions.

One night in the hospital, the tears streamed down my cheeks. "How can we teach our children resilience?" I cried. "It's all I want for my children!" I was acutely aware that children today need to be more resilient than ever before to brave the battleground of life. I was also conscious that resilience had gotten me through the tough days and that my optimism and confidence had served me well in life. If I could set my kids up with resilience, optimism, and confidence, I felt they'd be right in life. A nurse walked in and questioned why I was upset. I sobbed, "I want to know how to build resilience in my children. What can I do to set them up for life, emotionally?" She shot a silent worried look at my partner and then tried to reassure me. "Perhaps that's not a question to deal with today, just days after you've had a baby," she responded with both concern and a friendly smile. I nodded, but the question persisted in my mind, and it still does today. Although I've decided the answer to my question is role modelling, having conversations, and creating support networks, I am still acutely aware of the importance of resilience, confidence, and optimism, and I am anxious to instill these qualities in all out children, if we can.

About five months after I had the baby, I returned to work. I had a number of people seem surprised I was back so soon. In Australia, a lot of mothers opt to take a year off work, but I was ready to return to work, and as the sole breadwinner, I needed to. Plus, my partner was at home, so it was an easy transition back into the workforce for me. At home, there was never any question about my return date.

One of my more insensitive male colleagues turned to me and said, "The baby will prefer your partner" and "One day the baby will wonder who you are." I asked him if his children wondered who he was, as he was someone who'd worked fulltime while his children grew up. He said "no," since he was a father after all! This angered me. One day he even said to me, "The baby will think your partner is the mum!" I glared at him and then responded, "She is the mum." The two-mum thing seemed to bother him. I recognised it was probably a cultural difference, as he was from another country, although it had never seemed to worry him with our other kids. He was only bothered because I was now a biological parent. The truth of the matter was that, in part, we had made the decision that I would carry the child because my partner was at home with the children. This situation worked for us, and no one else's opinion on the matter mattered.

This baby is now nearly seven, and the love between him and my partner is fierce. She's his primary carer, and she's the first to admit she'd babied him—we had intended for him to be the youngest of the family, after all. My partner is the person he wants for everything. When she goes out for an evening, I'm the next best thing, but I'm never the preferred option to help him with anything. I wanted them to have a strong connection, and they do, which delights me. As he's getting older, this parental preference issue is reducing. The other day, we were at a party, and he called for me. "Mama," he said and grabbed my hand. "I want to show you where the dog is," and he took me to a dog in his kennel. It was a simple moment, but I was thrilled he had chosen to take me with him. I don't want him to prefer me, but I do enjoy him choosing me from time to time.

We're close, but he still calls for Mum much more frequently than he ever calls for Mama. A lot of nonbiological mums experience this, and they presume there's some magical biological connection that results in this closeness. I'm here to tell you it's nothing to do with biology. Nothing. In our case, he prefers his nonbiological mum because she has been his primary carer. So I shake my head when I hear this question about connection and say, "It's not biology; it's time and parenting roles."

Or it could just be a preference based on something entirely different. It's just definitely not biology. Externally, I'm more feminine than my partner, and our son often says something like, "Boys and tomboys over here, and the girls over there." He seems to see something in his mum that he doesn't recognize in me—perhaps, a reflection of himself. Our eldest son also feels this draw towards Mum over Mama; they talk video games, ball games, and so on. But when he wants to talk about books, writing, or his friends, he turns to me. It's funny because when we began this parenting journey, I asked my partner how we could differentiate our parenting brands for the children, given we were two mums. She thought I was crazy, but I am a marketing academic. Differentiation is key! I didn't know it at the time, but we didn't need to differentiate ourselves, as the kids chose our brands for us. I'm the parent they come to if they want to cook, talk books or writing, or sneak sweets! I'm the parent that's always saying, "Let's have a conversation about it." (My eldest son responds, "I don't really love conversation.") One of our daughters comes to me whenever she wants her hair done or help selecting a dress from her wardrobe. My partner is the parent they come to if they want something fixed, want to do jigsaw puzzles, or want to play a new video game or build Lego. But most of all, we're a big, happy family, and there are times that we just do it all together. We love to travel. We love to dine out. We love to visit family and friends. We love our family walks, or just playing or dancing in the house, and we all love to swim.

As a parent, I sometimes still feel that I don't really fit in. I don't fit in with normal mothers' groups because I'm not a traditional primary-carer mother. I don't fit in with fathers' groups because I'm not a father. I don't fit in with my childless friends because I have a large family of children. We don't necessarily fit in with foster carers and adoptive parents because we also have biological children. I suppose we do fit in with other people in two-mum families, but because our families are so planned and intentionally created, it seems rare for them to have more than two or three children, so again I still don't feel that we necessarily fit in. Occasionally, we come across a two-mum family with biological and fostered kids, and a lot of them, and I do feel a sense of fitting in.

But, ultimately, it doesn't really matter. We don't need to surround ourselves with only clones of ourselves. I do love diverse families around our kids. Luckily, the people around us do accept us for who we are, and I get joy in meeting and seeing lots of different families, and how they operate.

At some point the foster care agency said that they didn't have enough carers and needed people to provide short-term homes for children. We put our hands up and did another type of care—for over thirty children in two years. We're still on the list, although thankfully our phone rings much less often than it did before. It was interesting providing another type of nonbiological parenting for anywhere from one night to up to two years for a child, and our family makeup was always changing. It was a crazy and busy couple of years!

Recently, we had another addition to our family. I carried once again, but we waited until they were all at school fulltime before having the next baby. I wanted to be able to have just one child at home to focus on, something we had never experienced. This time I fell in love with the baby during the pregnancy, probably because we had already birthed a child and I knew what to expect when I held that baby in my arms or, perhaps, because I had a much easier pregnancy. I somehow loved someone I didn't know, which was a feeling I had never anticipated. Again, the love isn't different, just the timing.

Every so often the children ask my partner if she wished she'd carried a child, and she says "No, absolutely not." She doesn't feel she's missed out at all. Biology does not matter. Love is all that counts.

Chapter Ten

Of Children and Choices

Claire Candland

T he sun slides down the sky behind us, and a ghostly children's moon hangs before. My car zips along the freeway, windows rolled down slightly letting in the spring air. Playing on the iPod is "Another Train" by The Poozies. (It plays a lot these days.) As I drive, I'm singing with a strong voice: "You feel you're done, but there's no such thing/ though you're standing on your own, your own breath is king/ The beginning is now, don't turn around/ Regrets of bad mistakes will only drain you." Four-year-old Olivia is singing along in the back seat, kicking her feet to the beat. Eight-month-old Jasper is raising his voice with us—an unformed, untuned holler of joy for the sheer love of the sound. All three of us bright and singing, singing.

***

When I met Sloane, I was in the process of formulating a five-year plan that involved going to grad school and having a child—not necessarily in that order. I was twenty-five, and I'd already given up the idea of finding a life partner, but then suddenly there was Sloane. I let myself fall in love with her because she told me that she would be willing to move out of state with me for graduate school if I got into the program of my dreams and because she said she'd love to help me raise the children I wanted to give birth to. As we had adventures together, however, she kept telling me she didn't feel ready to parent, and I felt as if I was on hold waiting for her to be ready to start a real life—our life as a family with children. She finished her bachelor's degree. I applied for and was accepted into a master's program. We adopted a dog. We fought. We made up. We had a commitment ceremony in the

117

mountains with a live band and toasts to our future. I bought a house and put her name on the title. We travelled more; we fought more. The fights grew more traumatic and difficult to predict, but I blamed myself and my inexperience at committed relationships. I felt grateful that she put up with me despite all the ways I angered her. We drove overnight to get married in San Francisco during that brief time they were granting marriage licenses there. She told me that my parents were controlling and my family was unbearable. My parents told me that they worried she was making my life harder and that I should consider ending the relationship. Instead, we adopted a second dog.

And then, finally, Sloane said she was ready for a baby. But rather than my getting pregnant, she thought she should get pregnant. I am a couple of years older than she is, but she had a job with the state with excellent health insurance, whereas I was a graduate student with no health insurance at all. Given that we lived in Utah, where adoption of children by gay couples, even a stepparent adoption, was not possible, we thought that unless she had actually given birth to the child she wouldn't be able to provide the baby with insurance. And with my plan of finishing my master's degree and moving on to a doctoral program, who knew when I'd have any insurance at all to give to a child. Relying on state assistance for health insurance for a planned child was immoral and irresponsible, she said, and I ended up agreeing. So, she would get pregnant first, and I would get pregnant second.

I agreed to use a known donor because Sloane felt strongly that every child should have access to information about where they come from genetically; such information shouldn't be secret or a life-long mystery. Plus, it was cheaper and meant that rather than have our child be a product of a medical procedure, strictly timed and sterile, we could inseminate when it felt right, in moments of love and generosity. After a few months of asking around and looking for the right person to help us out, Alastair, a new friend of Sloane's, offered to donate semen. With his offer, I discovered that I had a requirement of my own: He had to be willing not only to be eventually known but also to become an actual part of our chosen extended family. Alastair is Black, and as a white woman, it did not feel right to bring a biracial child into this world only to cut them off from their Black family. This Sloane agreed to. Alastair agreed, as well, and we drew up a donor contract with the help of the woman who would, after a few years and a divorce, become his wife. We were warned that such a contract might not be enforceable, but we all felt that at least it would guide our interactions and speak to our intent. It reflected the best of all three of us and our hopes for the children to come.

When we found out that Sloane was pregnant, it was a brilliantly sunny December afternoon. Sloane called everyone she knew to give them the news that she was six-weeks pregnant; I left her to her joy and went and cried in the backyard where she couldn't hear me. The baby I'd very much wanted was coming but not through my body as I'd always hoped. That was hard enough. Making it harder was that the baby was coming through the body of someone I increasingly felt unsafe and mistrustful around. I cried because I was trapped by the love I already felt for a child who would likely never legally be mine. After I cried, I took a deep breath, reminded myself that I'd helped create this reality, and went inside to get ready for the graduate school holiday party we were attending that night—the party where we'd tell everyone our exciting news while we danced to OutKast's "Hey Ya!"

***

When we started trying to conceive a child, we didn't personally know any other lesbian couples, let alone lesbian parents. Oh, we had heard tales of such wonders, but as for real-life role models, we had none. I felt completely unprecedented as the female partner of a woman trying to get pregnant. And I was treated as if I were, too.

I went to every doctor's appointment, every test, and every ultrasound. I went to the birthing classes where the instructor referred exclusively to fathers when talking about the partner of the person giving birth. I read books on expectant fatherhood and couldn't find myself in those pages. I experienced couvade: I gained weight, had cramps, experienced hair-trigger emotions, and possessed a fully-fledged nesting instinct; my breasts also grew sore. We met some lesbian mothers, but they were biological moms and single and had nothing nice to say about their former partners, and none of those absent nonbiological mothers were around to parent their children. Because these new acquaintances held authority as so-called real lesbian mothers, those women, and their dismissal of the partners who helped them get pregnant, did more to undermine any sense that I was as much an expectant parent as any of the straight people who surrounded us.

***

Olivia is two months old, and I am exhausted. My new job as a receptionist for a federal regulatory agency started just two weeks after Olivia was born. As the lighter sleeper, I'm the one who most often wakes when Olivia does in the night. I have gotten the night-time bottle routine down pat, but my sleep schedule is broken, and my work schedule is rigid. As Sloane starts talking about her perception of our issues with our new couple's therapist, I zone out, counting the fern fronds on the wallpaper border around the room. I snap to attention when Olivia, still in her car seat in front of my chair, vomits, wakes, and starts crying. With the ease of practice, I unfasten the buckles, wipe away the mess, take off the bib, put on a clean bib, lift Olivia onto my shoulder, and start bouncing and rocking her back to sleep. Her fingers clutch at my hair and her body relaxes. Sloane hadn't even paused her monologue.

"You seem really comfortable with the baby." It takes me a minute to realize the therapist is talking to me. I look up at her, confused.

"What do you mean?"

"I mean you just took care of her so smoothly."

"Well, she's a spitter. I do this several times a day."

"Oh, I thought your intake paperwork said that Sloane was the mother."

I look at this queer woman looking at me in slight puzzlement. I know that she herself is a nonbiological mother of a son, so I don't understand why she seems surprised by my mothering my child.

It's Sloane who speaks. "I am the one who gave birth, but she's the one with the most experience with kids. She worked in daycare for ten years. She had to teach me how to hold the baby without dropping her."

For a moment, I'm grateful to Sloane for standing up for me, and then I'm angry that it's necessary at all. I realize that this woman is not going to be helpful to us as we struggle and settle into mothering together, and I stop listening to her entirely and just focus on my child.

***

Outside of legalities, what constitutes motherhood seems to fall into one of two paradigms for people: motherhood as an inherent, indelible fact inscribed by biology and/or pregnancy and motherhood as a status that is earned. The battle for supremacy between the two positions is a nasty one and takes no prisoners.

Yet in the lesbian household where one woman is the genetic or gestational mother and the other is a mother through intention and choice, these two paradigms coexist. It can be unsettling. Who is the so-called real mother here? More importantly, though, it can make the comothers feel at odds with each other in a scarcity-fuelled battle over territory and (emotional) goods, especially in the absence of any legal protections for the rights of the mother by choice. As the child-birthing mother nurses and coos and basks in the glow of accomplishment, the mother who didn't birth can often feel like a mother-in-waiting. She isn't a mother until she's earned it and proved it, until she has changed enough diapers and wiped enough noses and taken enough rectal temperatures. She isn't a mother, according to many, until she's proved not only that she is an indispensable part of the child's life but also that she has the kind of unique bond with the baby that supposedly only a mother could have.

There are only so many moments for the baby to get to know you. And for me, it felt like I needed to get in there and earn my motherhood pips right away. In the back of my mind was the thought that if anything happened to Sloane before I had earned my motherhood, anyone could come and sweep my child away with a claim of unfitness and lack of biological connection. Surrounded by these fears and outside opinions, it was, at times, hard for me to remember that Sloane and I were supposed to be cooperating, not competing. Sloane's need to control every decision reinforced these feelings in ways that were difficult to point to and discuss, but that left me feeling shaken and unsure that she herself recognized me as much of Olivia's mother as she was. We would fight and I would think about leaving, but I knew that without an adoption, my relationship to Olivia was too precarious to risk. I started trying to get pregnant myself as soon as I could, as I thought that if Sloane could feel what I feel and see what I saw when it came to motherhood, then perhaps together we could change those dominant models of thought and create a new paradigm—one that doesn't work through survival of the fittest.

***

I am concentrating on my breath. When I breathe in, I imagine that I'm pulling strength up into my body as a green sap. I see the sap flowing around the pain that pierces from between my shoulder blades through to my breastbone and radiates down my arms. On the exhale, the sap surges up and out of the top of my head, making me a fountain; love, pain, and power cycle through me with each slow breath. The tattoo artist needling a compass rose into my back seems unaware of what is going on inside me, but Fern, my oldest friend, sometimes squeezes my trembling fingers; she chose to be here with me because she knows what I'm doing and why. This tattoo is a spell to bind my child to me.

At the centre of the compass rose are three runes twined together as a bind rune: my, Sloane's, and Olivia's first initials. The north arrow hits a nerve and electric pain staccatos into my skull. I stay still and silent. Using skills I learned from the hypnobirthing class Sloane and I took three years ago, right before Olivia was born, I accept the sensation and push it up and out with a wish for years together with my daughter. In this moment, it doesn't matter to me if magic is real or if spells are effective; it's the choice to alter myself, to choose this particular pain, which carries the power in this moment. This moment makes my choice to parent Olivia through unknown territory indelible. No matter what storms come, her welfare will guide my movements.

Sloane thinks the tattoo is pretty.

***

I'm not the one who got pregnant with our second child.

After months of at-home inseminations, I sought help from a doctor. My cycles were super short, between thirteen to fifteen days, and had been my entire life. Ultrasounds, blood tests, hormone levels, and invasive procedures became the measure of my months. I did everything short of IVF to get pregnant. At between $10,000 and $15,000 a try, in vitro was out of reach financially, and Sloane didn't think we should use resources to get me pregnant when we knew she could get pregnant easily. Finally, I found a study that would make a shot at IVF as cheap as $3,000. I was accepted into the trial. We were wrestling with what to do about the fact that the clinic wasn't willing to use fresh sperm from a known donor; rather, it wanted to use frozen sperm from an anonymous donor or fresh sperm from a husband. Could Alastair and I just say that we were married? Should we actually get married just for the IVF trial and then get divorced? What were the legal ramifications of that? Should we just accept that the kids would not be genetically related at all and choose an anonymous sperm donor for the IVF trial? These were the current discussions when Sloane came home one snowy evening saying that she'd felt like she was ovulating so she'd stopped by Alastair's house on the way home from work and inseminated.

"What about my doing IVF?" I asked her. I was incredulous that she'd made that choice without talking to me.

"You know it's not going to work anyway. Why are we wasting more time trying to get you pregnant when we could be increasing our chances by inseminating me?" She puttered around the kitchen, gathering things for a salad, not meeting my eyes.

"But if you get pregnant?"

"You can still do the trial." She pulled down a soup bowl and made herself a salad in it. "If you manage to get pregnant, then we can be pregnant at the same time."

That was something I was unwilling to risk. Sloane was volatile and had been difficult to please during her pregnancy with Oliva; there was no reason to think she'd be different now. Our toddler was demanding; my work was inflexible. I hoped she wouldn't get pregnant. But two months later, right before it was time for me to start hormones for the IVF trial, she had a positive pregnancy test. After a couple of days of deep thought, most of it while wrapped in a thick cardigan and lying in a hammock trying to find warmth in an early spring sun, I made a painful phone call and dropped out of the trial. A month after that, Sloane had a miscarriage. After the miscarriage I told her I wanted to see if I could get back into the IVF trial, but she was adamant that she needed to get pregnant again in order to heal from the grief of the miscarriage. "You don't know what it's like to be so betrayed by your body," she said. "I need to prove that I can do this." I wondered what she thought my infertility had felt like to me, if not a betrayal by my body. Eventually she got pregnant again, and I just stopped talking with her about IVF.

***

Sloane and I learned about her first three pregnancies together. I learned about Sloane's fourth pregnancy in a text message she sent me from another room of the home we shared. We'd separated about six weeks before, and she'd moved into a bedroom in the basement. Our plan was to continue living together until Jasper (then five months) was at least two years old, but this news changed that. She texted: "I don't know how to tell you this, but I'm pregnant. Alastair is the father. He and I are going to raise the baby together." I was working evenings and weekends and telecommuting during nap times so as to be home in the day taking care of my children. Although Sloane was pregnant with a baby she said would not be my child, not only did she plan to continue living in my house, but she wanted me to add caring for the new baby to my routine. When she explained this great idea to me, a morning or two after her text announcement, I stared numbly at her until a bitter chuckle from my own throat caused me to blink. I'd had friends lose their children during a separation from their partners because their partner, their children's biological mom, had claimed they were only roommates or nannies. If she could claim I was only a babysitter to one, she could claim I was only ever a babysitter to all of them. I also knew that if she was living in my house, I'd be taking care of that baby whether I intended to or not. Even in the short time we'd been separated, more than one of the nights she was responsible for Jasper, I'd woken to find him crying in my bed where she'd placed him because she'd wanted to get more sleep.

"I'll pay you. We can make this work," she tried to catch my eye, as I turned my attention to my computer and resumed my Bejeweled game.

"Nope." Jewels shivered and sharded on the screen.

"You're a piece of work," she bit out, and slammed the front door behind her.

Before I told her she had to find her own place to live, I hid the chef's knife she'd once stabbed into the bathroom wall during a fight. She stomped as she stormed around and the hardwood floors groaned. She reminded me that the children were hers, and if I made her leave, she'd take them with her. I was afraid of her temper all the time, but during pregnancy, her violence was always simmering, sometimes boiling over into ultimatums, threats, and physical violence against the house, objects, and me. At five-months pregnant with Jasper and in a fit of anger at me, she choked me and punched me in the face. The police were involved in this incident, which resulted in her being charged with domestic battery, despite her initial report that I'd been the attacker and the marks on my face were the result of her defending herself. She threatened to take the children and move to Texas if I cooperated with the police and the district attorney, so I didn't; the charges were dropped, and I stayed with her. We projected an idyllic lesbian family facade that only my parents and siblings could see through. I left the children with her that last day we shared the house because I was afraid for my safety and I didn't want Olivia to witness that violence. I was also terrified of the consequences of more police involvement.

I went to friends and sobbed in a heap on their dining room floor. When they needed to go to bed, I called my parents and drove forty minutes to get a few hours of broken sleep in their guest bed. Together, we planned for my and the children's safety—a plan that we knew had no legal standing. I woke before dawn and drove to my house. Sloane was still asleep. I packed bags for me and the children and then I walked downstairs. I told her I was taking Olivia and Jasper and staying with my parents until she moved out. I expected a fight, but she grunted at me, rolled over, and fell back asleep.

This would be our pattern for the next couple years. If I did something that angered her, she'd tell me that I was never going to see the children again. I would cry hysterically, dry my eyes, and choose to brave her anger and risk the pain of being denied my children by showing up to collect them at my scheduled time. She'd say nothing about her threats and pass the children over to me. I wrote stories about stolen children and then deleted them all, afraid that by writing them, I'd make them come true. We went to mediation and came up with a nonbinding agreement for custody; she violated it constantly, and I said nothing because there was nothing to say, no legal recourse. I was lucky to have the children at all. She spread lies about how I'd cheated on her, stolen money from her, and physically abused her; whenever she heard that I might have said anything about the conditions under which I was coparenting with her, she retaliated with threats and intimidation. I thought a lot about driving away, about not showing up, about resuming my graduate career in a state far away, and leaving the children behind along with all the trauma. My pain, though, was never greater than my love for them. In the end, I always chose to show up.

***

The day Louisa was born, Sloane dropped the children off to me and announced that she felt like she was going to have an emergency C-section that day. I nodded noncommittally and wished her luck. Later that afternoon, I got a text informing me that the child had been born and asking me if I could bring Olivia and Jasper to meet their sister. When we arrived at the hospital room, Alastair and his wife, Mara, excused themselves to go get something to eat. I helped Olivia into an armchair and put the baby in her lap. There were baby-name books scattered around and names scrawled on the treatment whiteboard. Sloane looked well enough for having had an emergency C-section, but she seemed agitated.

"How's it going?" I asked, carefully.

"We're having a hard time agreeing on names, but I think we may have finally settled on Louisa."

"Oh, ok."

"Things aren't actually going all that well." Sloane stopped and looked at me intently. "We had a fight in the delivery room; they tried to prevent the baby from getting her immunizations and the vitamin k shot."

"You didn't discuss immunization before the baby was born?"

"No. I didn't realize we had such a difference of opinion. They also told the nurses that the baby isn't allowed any formula supplements."

"They know that you didn't produce enough milk to feed either Olivia or Jasper, right?"

"Mara thinks that if I take goat's rue and just stick with nursing a little longer, no supplementing, I'll be able to nurse this time."

"She does, huh? Well, good luck with that."

"I'm realizing that I don't want to coparent with them. I'd like you to help me raise her."

I managed to keep my expression unchanged as I looked at her, thoughts racing. I could only imagine how stressful it must have been to be in the middle of a C-section and have to fight to have your child immunized—to be told that you can't choose how to feed your baby and that you are not an authority on your own body. I know that kind of erasure and powerlessness. For a moment, I softened. And then I filled with fear, which was quickly followed by rage. She had made a promise to Alastair to parent this child with him, and she couldn't just change her mind like that. She couldn't do to him what she'd threatened so many times to do to me, and I couldn't participate in that. I said that I'd only parent the baby if she, Alastair, and I all sat down together and agreed to such a change. She told me he'd never agree to that. I insisted that it was the only way such an agreement could work. She asked me to take Olivia and Jasper and leave.

***

I am sweating in the shade on my new back deck. Olivia, Jasper, and I have just moved into a new home, and I've spent this late-July afternoon setting up the turtle sandbox. We have been talking about different family structures. Olivia is five, almost six, and surprisingly uncurious about the differences between families. Aside from that conversation on Louisa's birth day, Sloane has refused to discuss with me a plan for how to talk to the kids about the complications of our family structure. How do we explain that they have two moms and no father, whereas their baby sister has a mom, a stepmom, and a dad? I have no idea what to say about that. So far, Olivia has not asked. This disinterest in family structures is different than what I've witnessed in Olivia's peers and the children I knew when I was a preschool teacher, but it is in line with Olivia's otherworldly, artsy, neurodiverse self, although it will be a few years before she and Jasper are diagnosed as on the autism spectrum. But at this moment, all I know is that so far, we've been lucky in her lack of questions. This conversation about families mostly involves my thinking aloud to myself in their company, looking for clues about how I should proceed.

I've mostly been treating Louisa like a niece, parallel to the way that Alastair is socially Olivia and Jasper's uncle. I've spent most of the past nine months second guessing this choice and trying to figure out what exactly an aunt would do to support Sloane and Louisa without compromising my own relationship with Olivia and Jasper. Mara watches Louisa during Sloane's workdays, but I'd kept Louisa for a few days when Sloane was fighting with Mara and wanted to undermine Mara's complacency around her role with Louisa. I felt bad about that, but refusing a request of Sloane's has consequences I can't always predict and don't always want to pay.

As I am sweeping up sand, Olivia looks up and says, "Mom, did you know that Louisa has three moms?" My heart sinks. In the past year and a half, Sloane has introduced the kids to two new girlfriends she insisted they call "mom." I speak in a carefully even tone. "Oh really, honey? Who are Louisa's moms?" "She has my other mom, she has Mara, and she has you. Only you don't love her enough to let her be around."

I feel the same type of mental swirl that usually precedes a migraine. "Honey, I'm not Louisa's mom, I'm her aunt, remember? I'm her aunt, just like how Alastair is your uncle." "No," she says. "You're my mom and Jasper's mom. She's our sister. That means you're her mom, too. But you don't love her like you love us."

And she runs off to swing on the swing set as my hands start to shake. When I text Sloane about what Olivia has just said, "I always told you that you could parent her" comes a few moments later.

***

I've given a lot of thought about what makes a mother or, rather, what makes a parent of any stripe. I've come to the conclusion that what makes a parent is the kind of inchoate love that spurs you to leap between your child and a rampaging semitruck—the kind of love that pulls you from your bed at night, over and over, night after night, to provide some need to that child; the kind of love that finds you spending hours reading *If You Give a Mouse a Cookie* or singing the *Gummi Bear* song just to bring them joy.

This kind of love isn't earned like a badge. This kind of love doesn't necessarily come from a pregnancy or birth. This kind of love comes from a choice to open oneself up to it. It comes from a choice to embrace the responsibility and vulnerability that make up a parent and a commitment to follow through on that choice, even when the effects push you into a life that you never expected or wanted. This kind of love is chosen over and over, and it remains a part of you, even if that child is later ripped away by death or circumstance or deliberate hate in any form. That love, that choice of openness, is what makes both adults equally a parent when the child makes its entrance into the world, no matter what role each adult is playing in that entrance.

It's a messy notion, I know, that no other qualification makes a parent but a choice to love. But then, messes and children go hand in hand. After all, parenting is a radical act of faith in the future, of love in the making; it is carried out one messy choice at a time.

***

I have been lying for hours in my canvas hammock in the shade of the huge elm tree in my backyard. It is just a couple of days after that text conversation. The shade is nominally cooler than the house. The canopy is so thick that I can catch only brief glimpses of blue as the leaves flutter in a gentle wind I can't feel down below. I feel miniscule, able only to see a small part of the sky, of the tree, of my life stretching before and behind. This Saturday as I feel so small, I am thinking of children and choices.

It has become clear to me that the choice that is best for my two children is to agree to raise their sister, as well. For the past eighteen months, I have strived to create a stable life as counterpoint to Sloane's chaos. I have cancelled dates, postponed trips, taken on a second job, and provided daycare in my home, all so I could be free to catch the kids when Sloane lets them fall. I have the children every day that Sloane works as well as many weekends and evenings. At my house, the routine is the same, and the bedtime never varies; there is a stable circle of family and friends, and no one I date ever meets my children, except as the most casual of friends. What I can see of my life moving forwards looks much the same. I am making myself look hard at this—a life where my two children have a refuge of safety and stability that they have to leave their little sister behind to enter, and she must watch her brother and sister abandon her over and over. I am imagining what that might do to them or what it is already doing to them.

I also know that I am already stretched thin; my budget has little room in it for error. Even so, I can, just barely, imagine being a single mother of three children. As I am not a legal parent to any of the children, there is no social safety net for me. One more mouth to feed is all I can do, and in this shadow-patterned moment I realize just how badly I want that additional mouth to come through my body. I am prepared for the idea of being a single parent of three only because deep down I've been expecting that as soon as I'm financially stable, I'll explore IVF.

Resentment rises, again, that I'm in the position, again, of being faced with the choice to put my resources towards parenting a child coming into my life in a way that erases my own hopes and dreams. Resting in a hammock under a towering tree, I feel sick both at the choice I am facing and at how terrible I feel for wanting to choose to walk away. The hammock sways for a long time. A translucent quarter moon passes through fragments of blue in the canopy above as I imagine letting someone else worry about and take care of Louisa. I want to hold onto my dream of pregnancy, birth, and parenting a child who may have my father's eyes, my mother's shape of face, or my grandmother's hands.

"There's no guarantee I could get pregnant anyway, though," I whisper to myself.

***

I have a theory about babies and souls. I believe that when a person is supposed to be in your family, their soul will find you, somehow. Your children will find a way to you through your body or another's, in infancy or when older. Over the years, I've shared this theory with very few people. It's not a particularly comforting theory, and it has problematic implications, I know. Sometimes, someone will say something like "well, no matter how bad Sloane was, you wouldn't have had your kids without her, so you must be a little grateful," and in these moments, I am glad for my facade. I'm convinced that if I'd chosen differently, if I'd gotten pregnant myself, or had a different partner that got pregnant, that I'd still have ended up with these children, my children. They'd have looked different, to be sure, but their souls would have been the same. I believe that they chose me to be their parent. To the world they may not look like me, but they look at the world the way I do, or, at least, they look in ways that are related to mine. It is clear to me and to those who see us together that my children and I are meant to be a family.

This, as much as I hate to admit it, is a very Mormon theory. Growing up in Utah, everything is saturated in religion and spirit. Until I moved elsewhere for a brief stint, I didn't know that it wasn't normal to ask a person's religious affiliation upon first meeting. My parents were Mormon apostates, so our extended family concentrated their desire to maintain the eternal family on me and my siblings. My parents might be lost, but part of them would live forever in heaven as long as we children remained faithful and true. My mother's younger sister used to stroke my hair during sacrament meetings when I sat next to her. She'd frequently tell me how I was supposed to be her little girl, but I was too impatient to wait for her. I was baptized at eight along with all my friends. I did it mostly to prove that I could and to make my aunt happy. As a teen I identified as a Wiccan. I marked the moon cycle with ritual and gave tarot readings to my classmates—spreading my cards out in crescents on the lunchroom tables. But I was always careful to keep my apostasy quiet at family gatherings. Mormons smile in the face of difference, but then they work to erase you when you're out of the room. Community is only as deep as your tithe and your outward appearance of conformity. I grew up seeped in stories about eternal families but conditional love.

I had coffee with one of the few people I've shared this theory with. He was listening to me spin my brain about parenting Louisa—the pros, the cons, the implications, the additional years coparenting with Sloane, the increased and problematic involvement of Alastair in my and my children's lives, as well as my resentment over Sloane's fertility and my confusion about what to do. As I slumped over and sullenly chewed on the rim of my paper cup, he took a deep breath, cocked his head, and said: "Weren't you the one who talked about how babies find their families? Maybe her little soul took the only path available to make sure she could be with you?"

***

Sloane and I worked out the details a few days after I agreed to the responsibility of coparenting Louisa, and Alastair told me he was fine with it in an awkward conversation at an event a few weeks later. I'd have Louisa when I had Olivia and Jasper, unless Alastair wanted to have her. To accommodate Sloan's new work schedule, I picked them up Sunday afternoon at 2:00 p.m. and kept them until Friday afternoon at 5:00 p.m.; they had dinner for two hours every Monday and Wednesday with Sloane. In the beginning, Alastair had her two overnights a week, but within a couple of months, he and Mara cut that down to just one overnight a week and then none. Instead, they chose to pick her up every Thursday morning for a three-hour playdate with another little girl they were watching.

Going from single parenting two children to single parenting three children, while working two jobs, knocked me completely off my feet. Olivia wasn't a difficult child, but her increasing challenges with school and social relationships had me preoccupied and puzzled. Jasper, who liked to figure out the worst-case scenario for any situation by direct experimentation, ran me ragged. Louisa just cried for weeks anytime I put her down. After a few months, she was finally secure enough that I could leave her playing happily on the floor while I prepared a meal or ran to the bathroom.

One afternoon, exhausted, I lay curled on my low bed. I thought about crying, but my eyes slid to a book I had begun reading before I started parenting Louisa, and I decided that was a better use of my time. I had to start over at the beginning. After a few moments, I heard a baby crawling towards me. There was no crying, though, so I ignored the sound and kept reading. The crawling sound came closer, and then a little baby head poked up between my two hands holding the book. My bed was no more than a mattress and box springs set flat on the floor, so it was easy for Louisa to climb up onto the bed between my elbows and stretch herself out. She was asleep within minutes, my book unavailable for reading beneath her puffy diaper, so I rested my head on her, too, and we stayed there together for a long while.

***

One January afternoon when the kids were two, three, and seven, I came home to a salted caramel latte emitting steam on my porch. Sloane texted that she'd left it there for me. I threw it away. A couple of weeks later, she stopped by with a bag of my favourite foods from the new Trader Joes that had just opened in our town. I took it from her suspiciously. A few days later, Sloane requested that I let her stop by to talk that evening. She wouldn't tell me ahead of time what she wanted to discuss, and, as usual, I didn't feel like I could refuse.

Her current relationship was fizzling out, and she wanted to talk about what it would look like to get our family back together. I looked out the window at the traffic on the street. I usually took shallow breaths around her because her cologne—the same that once upon a time I'd bury my head in her pillows to inhale—now always made me want to throw up if I breathed in too much of it. Today was no exception. It was snowing outside; the windows were closed, and I could barely breathe. I worked to keep my face smooth and my eyes kind. I do not remember what I said, exactly, but I know that I chose my words with care as I explained that there was no way I could restart our romantic relationship. After a few moments, she asked about moving in platonically. She said something like how we always made such great partners, as whatever we put our minds to we accomplished together; surely, we could try again to create that cohousing family we thought we could be before she got pregnant with Louisa? "No," I said. "No." A few moments later, I tried again to deflect: "How else can I help you and the children during this difficult time?"

She told me, then, that if I wouldn't let her move in, she'd have to reach out to Alastair and Mara and form a family with them because there was no other way she could afford rent for a house with a yard in the city. I looked around at my house with a yard in the city that I worked two jobs to be able to barely afford and back at her. She was looking at

OF CHILDREN AND CHOICES

me expectantly. She knew that I was cautious about increasing Alastair's role in Olivia's and Jasper's life. "If that's what you need to do," I remember saying into the terrible air, "then I hope it works out."

The immediate repercussion of Sloane moving in with Alastair and Mara was that she no longer had to rely on me for help with the kids. Living with them meant that when she was angry enough at me to withhold them, she had two other adults living with her to parent for her, although Alastair and Mara were only nominally more interested in parenting than Sloane. Although Louisa loved living with her dad, Olivia and Jasper continued to regard him as an uncle. When Louisa tried to tell them that he's their dad, too, because he's her dad, they would argue with her. "He doesn't act like a dad," Jasper would tell her. "He doesn't do dad things with us."

***

As I walk into the lunchroom at my kids' school where I teach kindergarteners, I see Sloane deep in conversation with the head teacher. Instantly, my breathing speeds up and my heart starts pounding. It is not unlike how I used to feel when we were first dating, but the thrill of excitement is now terror. Things have been tense since I informed her that I'd be moving in with Dani, the woman I've been dating for the past two years, and her kids from a previous relationship. Sloan had even had moments of open hostility towards Dani and the blending of our families. I focus on the children I'm helping. Jasper walks by with the other kindergarten class and gives me a quick hug before running out to recess. I continue to mostly ignore the women in conversation until Sloane approaches. She does not stop as she passes me, but she spits out words "The head teacher needs to talk to you."

I turn to the head teacher. She looks concerned. "What's going on?" I ask her.

"I got confused," she replies, "and I accidentally mentioned that Dani's kids will be starting here in the fall. I'm so sorry. I didn't realize that she'd be so angry."

"It's not your fault," I murmur and excuse myself to go back to my kindergarteners.

Fifteen minutes later an email from Sloane comes through on my phone. I open it with fingers that ache from tension and read the following:

133

Once again, I've been put in an awkward place and given a reminder that I am not coparenting kids with you. This shuffling kids back and forth between strangers is not in their best interest. You may have your Saturday to Wednesday as planned this week. Starting next week, we will switch to an every other weekend schedule, and we will share holidays. I will have them during the week, every week. I am the biological, legal, and now the custodial parent. I did not wish for it to come to this, but I have given far too many warnings.

I call the head teacher and have her find a substitute for my class, and then I go home early. I do not make it all the way to my car before I start sobbing.

***

Every time Sloane drastically changed the schedule or decided to keep the kids on a holiday that I was supposed to have, my friends and family would wonder what the children thought of the change. Eventually, many of them postulated, Olivia would notice and say something. But one aspect of Olivia's autism is that she lives in a constant present. She does not tell time nor does she keep track of schedules or dates.

Dani's kids do. They also have two moms and two homes; not only do they keep track of their own schedule, but they'd been keeping track of my kids' schedule, too. When I told Dani's kids that I couldn't get my kids as scheduled, they demanded to know why. I left it to Dani to explain. When my kids finally came for their weekend, Dani's kids were loud in their opinions about how little time Olivia, Jasper, and Louisa were getting to spend with us. I had negotiated an extra midweek night from Sloane, but the house was still way too empty for most of that summer, and finally Jasper, at least, had come to some conclusions.

After Sloane had taken the kids alone for a seventeen-day vacation, I got an email from her: "Jasper says he needs to spend more time at your house. I'm willing to discuss custody arrangements whenever you're ready." A mutual friend had told me that Alastair and Mara had done the bulk of the care of the kids over the summer and were tired of it. I suggested a joint custody scenario where I had the children Mondays and Tuesdays, Sloane had them Wednesdays and Thursdays, and we alternated weekends. After initially refusing, she agreed a week later to the schedule change, and for the first time since we separated, we had an equitable fifty-fifty custody split. There was no relaxing, though. I kept waiting for the other shoe to drop.

***

It's a grey January day when Mara shows up in my classroom. Sloane had told me a couple of weeks before that after almost three years, she could no longer stand to live with Alastair and Mara and was looking to move in with a friend as soon as possible. I had wished her luck. Now here is Mara trying to talk to me alone. Mara is bird thin and always in motion. As she speaks, she is even more agitated than usual. Her voice is breathy, and she stutters a little on some of her consonants.

"We want to make sure," she says "that no matter what happens, you don't lose any further time with your kids. It's clear to me and Alastair that they need you and your stability in their lives."

"What do you mean?" I ask her as blandly as possible.

"I mean that we're intending to seek custody of the kids. They shouldn't lose access to any of their family just because Sloane makes such poor choices."

"You're including Olivia and Jasper in your plans to seek custody?"

"Yes, but don't worry, we don't intend to actually take them from you. You've lost enough time with them already. But we do intend to make sure that Alastair's rights as a father to all three of them are protected. Sloane can't just choose to take our children from us. After we get full custody, we'll work something out with you."

I am being asked to trust them—to trust that these people, who couldn't be bothered to have their toddler for overnights and who had never supported Olivia and Jasper, would work something out with me after wresting custody away from both me and Sloane. Having Alastair forcibly removed from the children's lives, even Olivia's and Jasper's, is not something that I want; it is not in the kids' best interest, but neither is this plan. This plan is a power play based on revenge. If anyone can understand wanting to wreak justice on Sloane, I can, but I can't understand acting it out through the kids.

I reach out to Mara. I rest my hand on her upper arm and make myself smile to her face. "Thank you. I appreciate that. We'll work this out. Why don't you, me, and Alastair get together and compare notes?"

***

My goal was to keep Olivia, Jasper, and Louisa together as much as possible while maintaining or increasing the amount of time they spent at my house. Without consulting or informing any of them, I took our donor contract, a retainer, and the whole complex story to an extremely experienced queer family law attorney who thought that with the legalization of gay marriage and the granting of stepparent adoptions in our state that the law had finally changed enough so that she could help. Together, we crafted a strategy based on my and Sloane's annulled San Francisco marriage and the changing laws around gay marriage and queer adoption. The goal was to legalize my relationship to Olivia and Jasper through adoption and to Louisa through some sort of guardianship so that no matter how hostile Sloane and Alastair became, I had leverage and clout to fight for the best interest of the kids.

Sloane was sufficiently alarmed by Alastair's threats that she readily agreed to letting me adopt Olivia and Jasper. It took the combined effort of both my and her attorney to convince her that since she'd put Alastair on Louisa's birth certificate, and was collecting child support from him, that it was not going to be possible for me to also adopt Louisa. Three months after I scraped up the money for the retainer, I had signed adoption papers and new birth certificates in hand. I thought I'd feel better and safer now, but we were warned that a challenge to the adoption in the first year might be successful. My attorney clarified to me that such a challenge could come from Sloane, too, so I should continue to maintain my careful balancing act. After so many years I finally had what I'd wanted—a legally recognized relationship to Olivia and Jasper—but it felt hollow. There was no smiling picture with the judge. No parties. No jubilant Facebook announcement. There was only fear that the adoption could still be undone and the knowledge that Louisa's place in my family was just as legally ambiguous as ever.

The day of the adoption, both Sloane and I had to be present as well as Olivia and Jasper. My parents were there, too. Sloan insisted that Louisa join us. I took a picture of the three kids standing at the courthouse balcony, looking over into the entrance hall. In the picture, Louisa stands a bit apart from her siblings; her face is turned slightly towards them, her cheek a soft crescent of reflected light.

***

This time, the pain is in my left inner forearm. I place my feet flat on the ground and try to draw energy as sap into my body to surround the pain, but the visualization is hard to hold to. The sap rises, but it doesn't flow into my arm, and the pain resolutely stays backwatered. I watch as a line of fire in the form of a tattoo needle traces a flower with a labyrinth in its heart. The lines shift from purple to black and inflamed red, and from that into bleeding colour.

At the centre of this labyrinth is another rune, sibling to the one on my back, a bindrune made of the symbols for Olivia, Jasper, and Louisa. Over the years, I have not been able to shake the belief that somehow the binding spell in the tattoo on my back is the reason I still have my kids, despite everything. If I cannot bind Louisa to us through law, perhaps I can bind her to us through spirit, faith, and pain.

This tattoo hurts more than my first one. As the artist needles colour into my skin, I have to breathe through one petal at a time. Each time she starts a new petal, I tell myself that I will make it through this petal, and then I will make it stop, justify the lopsidedness, and call it finished. But I never say stop. Each particular moment is just barely what I can handle, yet each petal, each colour added to each petal, hurts more than the previous as my skin gets brighter and the blood seeps out faster. I am holding still, muscles taut with inaction; I trace the lines of the labyrinth with my eyes and, sometimes, send thoughts of Louisa and her siblings out into the universe on a ragged breath.

***

I started working on getting everyone to meet in mediation in an attempt to provide a permanent solution for Louisa. It didn't work; neither Sloan nor Alastair would compromise around Louisa or the other two. Alastair filed a challenge to the adoption 364 days after the judge had signed it.

***

There's something singularly painful about reading legal documents that reduce your role in your children's lives to something peripheral and functional. Alastair's legal motions stated on one page that I'd raised the children "practically since infants," but throughout the rest of the motion, the documents limited my involvement to childcare and school transportation. He stated that I'd only adopted Olivia and Jasper under duress. Sloane's attorney's responses focused on the language of the donor contract, and how despite plenty of opportunity for Alastair to provide substantive and emotional support, he had failed to do so. Reading them one might have thought that Sloane parented the children completely alone. My attorney and I held to our Switzerland strategy and refrained from offering our own perspective; we did just enough to assert my interest in the adoption but stayed clear from the animus being flung about.

Eight months after Alastair filed his motion to set the adoptions aside, we had a hearing before a judge, who dismissed the motion on the grounds that the donor contract remained enforceable and the adoption was in the best interest of the children. The victory felt, and remains, as bittersweet as the adoption itself. Olivia and Jasper are legally protected, but Louisa's situation remains ambiguous and undetermined.

Upon being served with notice of the lawsuit, Sloan started refusing to let any of the kids see Alastair during her parent time. The responsibility of supporting Louisa's relationship with her father has fallen entirely on me. I facilitate his relationship with Louisa during my parent time with her, against the express wishes of Sloan. Louisa frequently expresses a desire to spend more time with her dad during Sloan's parent time, which Sloan ignores. Every week during my parent time, Louisa faces the choice of seeing her family at her father's house or spending the full amount of time at my house with her siblings and the stepsiblings she loves. Sloane's ongoing unwillingness to collaborate on any front limits my options for mitigating Louisa's pain.

So, I continue to smile and facilitate transitions. I continue to advocate for Louisa's need to see her father more frequently and for Olivia and Jasper's need to sometimes see the man they consider an uncle. I continue to calm the flames when I can between the parties involved, although, at times, I feel more like spewing them from my eyes and mouth. For years, I had felt like Cassandra from the Greek myths, uttering warnings about where our choices were taking us and being constantly brushed aside. Now, though, I want my words to inflict that pain on others; instead, I meet Alastair and Mara for coffee and nod sympathetically when they complain about Sloane and their stolen children. I sit in Sloane's kitchen and shake my head while she rails about Alastair and Mara's delusions about their rights to Olivia and Jasper while fending off her threats to my relationship with Louisa due to my defiance of her orders not to let her see Alastair. In the end, it doesn't really matter what any of them think of me. I have achieved a legal relationship to two of my three children and have established a track record of being the only adult in this complicated family who has worked to facilitate the children's relationships with all the people they are attached to. It's a role I took on through choice after choice, and I wouldn't choose to change it now, just for the pleasure of letting them all know how I feel about them. Some truths are best served by silence and restraint.

***

It's late on a school night in the last week before summer break. My kids and Dani's kids all went to bed reluctantly, and it's just now that I'm getting to clean the kitchen up from dinner. The kids were creative in their stacking of their dirty dishes in the sink, and it takes me a bit of skill to pull out dishes and rinse them off without tumbling the entire pile or spraying the floor with water. As I work, I let some of my frustration come to the surface. Sloane has a new fiancée, and my kids are distancing themselves from Dani as they adjust to yet another new stepparent being forced on them. My eyes catch sight of Jasper's medication bottle on the windowsill, fuller than it should be, because Sloane keeps forgetting to give Jasper his ADHD medication. I begin thinking of all the ways things will be different when I can get full custody of my kids. I will be able to provide consistent bedtimes and homework routines more than half of the time. I'll be able to make sure Jasper gets his medication every night. I'll be able get Louisa back... into...

I stop.

My hand is in the centre of the stream of hot water.

I won't be able to do anything with Louisa. Not one thing. My attorney is confident that if I wanted to pursue full custody of Olivia and Jasper, I would probably succeed. But without anything legally binding Louisa to me, there is nothing to stop Sloane from refusing to give her to me, just as she frequently refuses to let Alastair see Louisa. If I win full custody, it seems I'd lose Louisa.

My hand starts burning, and I pull it rapidly back, still holding a plate, sending a cascade of hot water to the floor.

I look from my scalded hand to the rune in my labyrinth to Jasper's medication and beyond to the ornamental cherry tree outside, with leaves gilded by the sunset. There will be no attempt at full custody of Olivia and Jasper for the foreseeable future. My hand cools, and I finish the dishes and go to bed early.

***

Although I had chosen to love Olivia and Jasper before they were born, I fell in love with them at different times. I felt that first deep stir of primal love for Olivia when, moments after she was born, I said her name, and she turned her head towards me. Her eyes opened, and I fell into them and changed.

My love for Jasper was slower. His first few months were so emotionally fraught and the months after Sloane and I split up were so hard that sometimes the balance between resentment and love that (I hope) all parents sometimes feel was tipped more towards resentment. It wasn't until the first New Year's Eve, the closing of my first year as a single mother, when he woke up at 10:00 p.m. and kept me company through my vigil, sometimes crooning with me as I hummed songs into the silence, that the love grew brighter and clearer.

As much as I tried, though, I didn't love Louisa for a long time. It's hard to love a walking interrobang right away. I didn't love her until she trusted me enough to share her softer stories with me. One day, sitting with me on the porch stairs, she said this to me: "Mom, did you know that in the morning the sun is on this side of the sky, and it goes to the other side at night? And the moon does the same thing? And they dance around each other like they're in love. Because sometimes the moon is just a half, but sometimes it's a whole. Like the sun. The sun is always a whole. So sometimes the moon makes itself like the sun, and they spin together." She looked at me, and I looked at her. We then, together, looked up at the soft moon dancing in the sun's sky.

Works Cited

The Poozies. "Another Train." *Chantoozies*, Hypertension, 1993.

Chapter Eleven

Unnatural Parenting

Emily Regan Wills

My first baby was six weeks old, and he had blown out his diaper, again, while we were out at a nice restaurant in Manhattan. My wife, exhausted from the sleep deprivation of being the nursing mom, passed him over to me, and I carried him into the ladies' room, under the assumption that there was a changing table. There was not. No counter space. No clear space on the floor that wasn't constantly full of foot traffic. Even the tiny space between the two sinks had a hole leading to the trash can beneath it. Here I was, holding a squirming, shit-covered newborn who couldn't hold his own head up properly, with a diaper bag (which had, six weeks ago, been my laptop bag for hauling my stuff back and forth to grad school) over my shoulder, and I had no idea what to do.

I think every woman who came into that bathroom in the next fifteen minutes helped me. Someone balanced the changing pad over the space between the sinks; people handed me clean wipes from the package, took gross used wipes and threw them out, held the plastic bag open to deposit the gross sleeper, and cooed at my adorable baby who was giving them all extremely suspicious looks.

Just as I was getting him wrestled back into a new sleeper, a new woman came into the bathroom.

"Do you need a hand?" she asked.

"No, I think I've got it," I said, fighting a little floppy fist into a sleeve.

"Is that your baby?"

"Yes, it is," I said proudly.

"He's beautiful."

I beamed. He was, objectively, the most perfect infant ever.

"I agree."

"And you look great!"

I knew, in some part of me, that she meant "considering you just pushed a human out of your vagina six weeks ago," which I had, in fact, not done. But fuck it. I'd gone back to teaching when he was six days old. I deserved the ego boost.

"Thank you," I said.

Her voice dropped, conspiratorial.

"And your boobs look fabulous."

I glanced down at my boobs, which had grown along with the rest of me, as the combination of dissertation-proposal stress and holy-shit-my-wife-is-pregnant stress had sent me into a nine-month doughnut coma. They were not doing anything to feed the flailing baby in my hands. But they were, objectively, pretty fabulous.

"Thank you," I said, and snapped up his sleeper.

***

I am a second-generation hippie and feminist. Although I grew up in a pretty standard American suburb, with a dad working shift work and a stay-at-home mom, I also grew up buying food from the bulk bins at the local food co-op, having a favourite tofu recipe, and making hummus in the blender. Our dinner table conversations touched on gender equality, racism, my mom's experience as an antiwar organizer in the 1970s, and the need to protect the environment. My dad did housework, and my mom was the one who knew how to use power tools. And although my mom didn't work for pay, she was deeply involved in community work. Her two major commitments when I was young were to Intensive Caring Unlimited, which supports the parents of kids, like me, who were born premature and with medical issues, and to a breastfeeding support network she helped found.

I don't know what my parents called their parenting philosophy, or if they had an intentional one, but it resonates with much of what is called "attachment parenting" or "natural parenting" these days. I was breastfed until I was in preschool; in fact, when my mother told me she was going to stop nursing me, I was able to reply, "Mommy, why don't you love me anymore?" I wore cloth diapers back in the days when they involved physical pins. (Mine had duckies on them. I still have a couple.) I was worn in a Snugli everywhere as a baby, by my dad as well as my mom, and coslept with them intermittently into late toddlerhood. As I grew older, I was allowed to speak my mind and to have my opinions heard. I changed my brother's cloth diapers, too. To me, this was normal—this was how parents behaved and how families worked. When friends told me they got in trouble for talking back, I literally couldn't comprehend what they had done; when I first encountered disposable diapers as a preteen babysitter, I was mystified.

So natural, attachment, and antioppressive parenting was normal to me. What else would I do? This is how you parent, isn't it?

***

When I was fifteen, I was diagnosed with bone cancer. (Not osteosarcoma—a weird one, you haven't heard of it.) I was also starting to figure out what it meant to be queer. I had tried to come out the year before, in eighth grade, but it didn't go well. On my sixteenth birthday, I kissed my best friend at summer camp, and she kissed me back. I lay on the operating table six days later, ready to have my tumor removed and my legs reconstructed, entirely unsure whether I would wake up. I was a queer mess of a kid who wasn't convinced she would live to adulthood.

I spent the next few years in pain and in love; I forced my body and my mind through as normal a high school experience as possible. Everything for me was determination. I was going to get through this, and I was going to succeed. My girlfriend (because that's what someone becomes after you kiss them when you think you're going to die) learned how to load my wheelchair into the trunk of her '98 Ford Probe. An ex-girlfriend of mine started a gay-straight union and made me vice-president (which, in retrospect, was probably peak lesbian for me). My parents got okay with me being out, probably in part because it was the least of our problems. I walked down the aisle at high school graduation on crutches, wearing a rainbow tassel on my graduation hat.

Somewhere between having my legs carved up and putting that rainbow tassel on my hat, I sat in the doctor's office and heard my surgeon say that they'd cleared all the cancer out of my body, and that I wouldn't need chemo or radiation. I would, though, need to be monitored closely if I ever got pregnant because the growth hormones in my body might cause my cancer to come back.

That's okay then, I remember thinking. I'll just never get pregnant.

My girlfriend and I would fight about whether we'd have kids. (We were very weird seventeen-year-olds, or maybe we weren't.) She wanted to have two kids, the first before she turned 30, because she had heard it reduced your chances of breast cancer. I didn't want to have kids at all. Finally I said to her, "I don't know if I'll be a good parent."

"That's fine," she said. "I'll be a good parent, and you'll be fine."

It's twenty years after that conversation. Reader, I married her, and my ex-girlfriend was the photographer. We've got two kids. And let me tell you: I am definitely the better parent.

***

When my first kid was born, I was a grad student doing my first solo-taught course. I went back to teaching when he was six days old, leaving my wife home alone on her three-month-paid maternity leave—an absolutely brilliant perk of her great job. (Then the financial crisis came, and she was laid off. Her unemployment check was still larger than my grad school stipend check.) When we were broke, we applied for Medicaid for her and the baby, and then the Women, Infants, and Children (WIC) Food Program. I wasn't included in the family unit until after our second-parent adoption paperwork was completed, so I couldn't go in for Medicaid with them and had to keep paying the premiums on my school insurance. When we went to the WIC office, they weren't surprised at two women coming in together but asked who was the mom and who was the auntie. "We're both the moms," my wife said. "But she's the one on the paperwork," I said.

When my second was born, our family was living in Ottawa, the capital of Canada, where I'd gotten a full-time job as a university professor. Excitedly, I sat down to do the paperwork for Canada's vaunted, one-of-best-in-the-world maternity benefits, generally called "mat leave" by everybody. Except, the thing is, I wasn't eligible for it. Canada's fifty weeks of leave split between the parents begins with fifteen weeks of maternity benefits, which the website you use to apply for Employment Insurance describes as being "only available to the person who is away from work because they're pregnant or have recently given birth." The next thirty-five weeks are called parental benefits, "available to the parents of a newborn or newly adopted child" (Government of Canada). It's those weeks that can be shared between the parents; those were the weeks I was eligible to take. I squinted and muttered at the website, and then applied for my money.

After consulting with a lawyer and our families, we decided not to go through with a second-parent adoption with our second kid, our dual citizen, our tiny little Canadian. When it came time to apply for permanent residency in Canada, our lawyer's assistant asked us to clarify a few issues. Was our eldest child my adopted or biological child? What about our younger one? I looked at the adoption papers for the older child, and the unaltered birth certificate. "Well," I said. "Adopted for the first, biological for the second," I guess. And so that's what she checked off.

***

I remember sitting on the phone with one of my best friends. She'd woken up two years before from what was supposed to be a fibroid removal surgery to discover that she'd been diagnosed with uterine cancer and that she no longer had a uterus. She'd just been told she'd have to lose her last ovary and her last chance at biological motherhood. She was mourning the loss. And I was sympathetic, but the thing that I had trouble with was the idea of biological motherhood as a thing to lose. She could still be a parent—the kid just wouldn't have her DNA. Why did that matter? It was the work of parenting that mattered.

But then again, I hadn't understood why my wife wanted to get pregnant, four years earlier. I hadn't understood why it mattered to her that she grow a parasite in her body for nine months. Babies mattered, and I loved babies. I loved watching them grow and change and loved being able to love them with my whole self. But pregnancy meant giving your body over to a force beyond you. Even if the results are good and are what you want, that loss of bodily integrity for nine months seemed to me like the worst possible idea. I had given up my bodily integrity for three years to doctors, whose work was bloody carpentry, as they hammered and sawed at my limbs until they mostly functioned. Why on earth would anyone do that voluntarily?

My friend cried on the phone. I loved her, and so I listened. I repeated back what she felt but was mystified.

***

I am my mother's oldest child, but I am the product of her second pregnancy. My only full sibling is the product of her fifth. I only remember one of her miscarriages—the one that required hospitalization—but it's part of my history, a part I grew up with. Bodies betray us. That's a lesson I learned young.

***

When we moved to Canada, we sent our kid to an alternative, progressive public school, because we are hippies. Across the street from the school was a breastfeeding supplies store, featuring trendy nursing bras, clothes with well-designed easy-access slits, a full variety of nursing pillows, as well as a small and well-curated selection of carriers. (Not cloth diapers, though—the other good baby stuff store, owned by another mom of kids at my kid's school, had those. The two owners are friends, and I think there was an informal noncompetition agreement between them.) Once our second child was born, my wife began to go to a weekly breastfeeding support group there—not that she'd ever had trouble nursing, mostly just to meet people. Meanwhile, I joined the local baby-wearing Facebook group, in part because all the cool moms on the playground seemed to be in it. At the same time, we started going to playgroups for queer families. To this day, our friends in Ottawa can be neatly divided into friends from the alternative school community and friends from the queer families playgroup—my two most comfortable comfort zones as a parent.

For a long time, we were the only queers at the alternative school; most queers live closer to downtown, in a different school catchment. And we're really some of the only hippies at the queer families playgroup, which has a nice mix of radicals and assimilators, all working in a government town. It's not that I feel discriminated against or ostracized or odd. What I am is different. But when have I ever been anything else?

***

It's almost all moms on the baby-wearing group. We've done #mancrushmonday posts, in which everyone has a photo of their husband wearing their babies in a carrier. We get jokes about how much money the members are spending on woven baby wraps and how their husbands are mad about it. We share knowledge about which types of wraps and soft-sided carriers and which slings are best for nursing while still in the carrier, and about how to wear the first baby while pregnant with the second.

I post photos of my wife and me, taking turns with our baby in the sling, and say that it fits both sizes of mom in our family. Everyone clicks "like."

My wife takes me to breastfeeding club with her. I sit with the other moms and chat. I've never nursed a baby, and I never will. Nobody objects to me being there. Just being female, apparently, is enough.

I am never certain if I am the right sort of woman, if I am any sort of a woman at all. If it's a question of picking my team, though, I'm sitting on the girls' bench. Everyone else seems to think I am. In any case, I play along.

***

My mother kept a photo of my nephew holding my older kid on her desk at work. My nephew is my half-sister's son, with no genetic relation to my mother, just like my son. People would look at it and tell her how much they look alike and how much both boys look like her.

They do, you know. Somehow, they do.

***

Underlying hippie parenting practices is always the idea that it's natural. It's natural for babies to be held close, that they be fed breastmilk, that they are born via noninduced natural labour, and that they are kept away from chemicals and plastics that might harm them.

The thing is that there's nothing about me that's natural. I was born too early to breathe and survived because of tubes in my lungs. My legs are full of screws and plates and experimental grafts. My children, too, are unnatural; they were conceived via tubes of sperm shipped to me in dry ice and thawed in my lace bra and were born only with assistance from doctors with vacuums in hand. And in claiming the name queer, I link myself to a lineage of people who reject what they were told was natural for them—heteronormativity, the nuclear family, the Protestant work ethic.

Today I was reading Paulo Freire for work. (It's bloody great being an academic most of the time.) He describes how his "culture circles," the radical literacy teaching practice he developed, introduced the nature-culture distinction to illiterate Brazilian peasants. For Freire, "culture is all human creation," (44)—everything that exists between people and in the interaction between people and their environment. He quotes one of the participants in his culture circles, who describes a picture of flowers in a vase: "As flowers, they are nature. As decoration, they are culture" (71).

Natural parenting is not the flowers in the field because it can never be. We are creatures of culture, all of us, by virtue of being humans. We are the flowers in the vase, arranged, put together intentionally, because we see something beautiful and want to bring it into our home. Or more: my parenting is planting the flowers for the vase, ensuring that they grow strong and wild, making them ready to take their places, to come into the world and change it.

***

I yell to everyone that dinner's ready. My kids stomp up the stairs from their basement playroom, shouting about whatever game they were playing. My wife extracts herself from the couch where she has slumped after a long day of managing our high-energy, high-volume kids. It's summer, so our kids' auntie is here until she has to go home to prep for her next year of teaching high school; she tells the kids to go wash their hands. We set the tables: plates and silverware, juice and craft beer and bad summer wine. I put out the salad with the vegetables from the farmers' market, the homemade veggie burgers (black beans, rice, frozen corn, tamari, smoked paprika, in the food processor—it's pretty great, you should try it). Next week my eldest goes to sleepaway summer camp for queer kids and queerspawn; he's planning on spending the whole time up a tree. My youngest wants to know when we can go for another swim in the lake. I propose that maybe on the weekend we can do a hike and a swim again.

"No hike," he says with four-year-old petulance. "I hate nature."

"I know, baby," I say. "Eat your kale." And he does.

Works Cited

Paulo Freire *Education for Critical Consciousness*. Bloomsbury, 2013.

Government of Canada. "EI Maternity and Parental Benefits." Canada, 2020, www.canada.ca/en/services/benefits/ei/ei-maternity-parental.html. Accessed 16 July 2020.

Chapter Twelve

All the Ways We Didn't Have a Baby (and a couple of ways we did)

Stacy Cannatella

There were so many ways we didn't have a baby. I never could have imagined that one day we'd have three, sweetly snuggling like piles of puppies, showing off their wiggle dance moves, and giving unsolicited "I love yous." Due to my own childhood, there were a lot of things I never could have imagined. My usual repertoire of what-ifs only involved car crashes, terminal illness, and homelessness. But there are so many shocking surprises about children. That they shiver with excitement about rinsing with mouthwash. That they love each other. That they whisper to you late at night, "Mommy, I love your nose. I love your eyebrows. I love your black hair," as they gently poke you in the eye and ruffle your mostly gray hair. These possibilities had been beyond my stunted imagination.

Our kids are six and three and three now, but for years, there were many ways we did not have a baby. Each time we tried, I was sure: *This is it! This is how we're going to have a baby*. My mind would soften like warm, red wax, ready to have this memory imprinted on it like an official seal. I collected these memories for our future children, but now, I don't know where to put them. We're cleaning out the garage, and I wish I could pack up these moments in a box, with the outgrown tiny clothes and plastic toys, to give to someone who could use them.

I'm just old enough and lucky enough that I managed to avoid all forms of Internet dating. I met my wife the old-fashioned way, in this messy 3D world thick with pink sunlight, tumbling laughter, and rusty leaves fluttering to the earth. On the first day of our college orientation, I heard Cynara laugh at the next table. When I looked, I could not look away. It turns out all my neurons had receptors in the shape of her that had just been waiting in case we ever met. She was with someone else, so we became friends, crossing paths for years in academically green quads, under the glow of wrought iron lampposts, and on stone stairs worn down in the middle. We stayed up all night talking and woke up aching on historic divans with wooden arms under the glow of infomercials yelling about OxyClean and Jesus.

Years later, after we finally kissed, Cynara told me she could picture a bassinet in the corner of the bedroom. I squinted to see it. This was not a part of my childhood fantasies. When I was young, I fantasized about being the first woman to become a professional baseball player. Later, I fantasized about being able to pay for college, have my own apartment, or find a job that didn't make me cry every day. I vaguely thought I might have kids, but I assumed it wouldn't happen if I ended up with a woman. So, when she mentioned the bassinet, I followed her gaze and stared into the darkness until something started to materialize, blue and hazy, with a frilly hood. With Cynara, a future started to appear, rippling out from that kiss, where there was only a void before.

A year and a half after we got married, she said she thought we should start the process. "Now?" I asked. It seemed abrupt. I was thirty-five. Everything always seems abrupt to me. In the time it takes me to fold laundry and put it away with hundreds of tiny circular trips, she paints the basement, fixes a flat tire, and plans a vacation using a complicated system of points I don't understand. Cynara lives in a world that moves at a slightly faster speed than me, like a hummingbird or Charlie Chaplin.

Adoption: It isn't about you

First, we wanted to adopt. After all, there are so many babies, and I was not attached to my own twisted DNA. I wanted a baby I could love fully, the way I love Cynara, untainted by imagined reflections of myself. I was never someone who was into women's circles, moon cycles, or belly dancing. Fertility had always been an inconvenience: something that made my softball uniform too tight, made me cry at Hallmark commercials, and made me worry in high school when my period was late.

Cynara started researching with the fast-forward fervour she usually reserves for bargain hunting. She quickly established that private adoption cost more money than we made in a year, and most international adoption wouldn't have us. So, we signed up for a class to foster or adopt through DCF (Department of Children and Families). You have to learn a lot of acronyms when you're trying to have a baby. You don't have time for whole words. It started with DCF and TPR (termination of parental rights), before we even knew about TTC, TTWW, IUI, KDs, WTBK, and IVF.[1] You also have to meet a lot of people: social workers, families, and, of course, the children themselves. And you have to get all of them to like you. This made me twitch. I grew up in a family that was private like the KGB. I learned to be different with different people, so even at a friendly party full of people I know and love, I am in danger of spontaneous combustion. While I knew that Cynara and I alone in a room could never produce a baby with just the power of our love, I hadn't realized it would be such a crowded affair.

As we descended the tan, linoleum stairs into the DCF basement, my eyes dilated to let the image linger too long on my retinas. The light slid diagonally from the high windows to the floor, and the soft traffic of dust particles swirled upwards, illuminated, unfettered by time and gravity. *This is how we're going to have a baby.* I knew it would be expensive, long, and potentially heartbreaking. I knew we might not be chosen because we were gay or because our apartment was too small or because our houseplants revealed our inability to sustain the most basic form of life. I knew we might end up with children who were traumatized to the point where all of our love could help a little but never heal them completely. I was prepared for all this. But I was not prepared for the role plays.

Role playing makes my blood thicken like quick-dry concrete. Add an audience and my lungs stiffen until I can't breathe, as a prickly-red spreads over my body. In our class of twenty people, the social worker would introduce an improvisational role play about kids who stabbed their parents or smeared shit on their door. "Remember," she'd remind us, "This isn't about you!" We weren't sure if the plays were designed to weed us out or prepare us for our roles as foster parents. I tried to look invisible as the social worker described the parts (usually including some combination of a suburban white mom who knows nothing about her kids' cultures, an angry teenager threatening revenge sex-work, and an abusive teen boyfriend). I would study the industrial rugs in this DCF basement, worn down by role plays that never included babies or love. I would promise the godless universe that I would be the best parent in the world if I could just avoid being picked for this. I would suck in the air, dense with despair, and hold it. But I got picked. We all got picked. When the couple next to us tried to politely pass on the role play, the social worker said, "You can pass, but we're looking for participation. And we choose who gets a baby."

Before the home visit, we were advised to bake cookies to make the apartment smell like love. We piled our junk in closets and took it as a sign from the universe when our scraggly hibiscus bloomed for the first time in a year. We were hoping to have two kids, but as the social worker pressed the button to retract her metal tape measure, she informed us that our square footage would only legally allow us to foster one child.

Today, our three kids choose to share one small bedroom. Our oldest daughter, Julia, briefly had her own room, but she said, "It's not fair that I have to sleep by myself! Lea and Zoe sleep together, and you and Mommy sleep together. Why do I have to be alone?" Now, they sleep in a bunk bed, two snuggled on the bottom and one on the top, surrounded by legions of stuffed animals. I remember being an only child with my own room and fantasizing about secret rooms, attics, basements, and tree houses that would provide deeper and deeper solitude. Every day, I am shocked and delighted that my kids are nothing like me.

After completing the forms, the essays, the home visit, and the background checks, our final day of class was a panel discussion of parents. First, a woman in her sixties with a sensible straw-blond crossing guard haircut and a pink Patriots sweatshirt told us that "We wanted a baby girl to complete our family ... Long story short, we ended up with three teenage boys." She laughed. "Since then, we've fostered over twenty teenage boys. Some of them even keep in touch."

Next, a young dad explained how he and his wife had fostered a baby and adopted her when she became "legally free." "We raised her for a year and a half, but then ..." He trailed off and started to cry. Cynara and I grabbed hands under the table and squeezed. From the first day of class we knew that DCF's primary goal was reunifying biological families. But only our brains understood this, as we tried to balance the risk and weight of emotions we did not yet have. The dad explained that a previously unknown bio-aunt appeared out of nowhere, and the baby was given to her. "But we're good," he said. "After a year of therapy, we were ready to try again, and they matched us with a beautiful baby girl.

There is a bio-relative ... but we're still optimistic." He teared up and apologized for his wife's absence. Under the table, I stepped on Cynara's toe, and she pressed her thigh against mine, but we didn't look up. We didn't want the social workers to smell our hesitation.

We had recently gotten our dog, Cosmo, from the animal shelter. He had been found in a garbage dump in Puerto Rico and shipped to Boston. They stuck a needle deep into his heart to stop the heartworm that had left it full of holes. We wrote essays, got references, documented our landlord's approval, and paid hundreds of dollars to bring him home. I knew it was offensive to compare a dog to a child, but I tried to imagine how I would feel if someone took him away. Then I tried to multiply that feeling by a factor of human. When we got home from class, we put our official foster/adoption classwork and certificates on a shelf in a closet. We both knew we would never touch them again.

Frozen

A few months later, we started sifting through sparkling profiles of sperm that had been clinically extracted, tested, washed, and frozen. Soon, we were crinkling into stiff paper dresses and putting our legs up into metal stirrups, shined and chilled under fluorescent lights. We took turns pushing the small plastic plunger that always went wavy through optimistic tears.

When you buy sperm, there is a menu. Each vial (roughly 1/8 of an ejaculation) costs about the same as rent. The purchase comes with the donor's medical history, essays, and "office impressions," supposedly written by the people who handed the donor his forms, cups, and porn. The "office impressions" read like personal ads with a focus on hair and teeth: "Donor 34792 is truly a Prince Charming with wavy blond hair, dreamy blue eyes and a smile that warms your heart. When he is not trading stocks or doing yoga, he enjoys running marathons." For an additional fee you can buy the donor's baby pictures, essay, audio recording, or creative submission. We started out wanting to buy all the information; we were looking for someone kind, smart, and funny (even though we knew none of this was genetic), but by the end, we were fantasizing about paper grab bags of bargain-basement sperm.

We were in love with our first donor. He loved his grandma, he loved Madonna, and he loved to dance. His essays made us feel like he was someone we would have dated or at least gone clubbing with in the 1990s. The sperm came in a brown, cardboard box that came up to my thigh, where I developed a bruise from bumping into it in our hallway. Surely, a box so big should be filled with buckets of sperm. But inside that box was a thick metal tank filled with dry ice, surrounding two thin vials smaller than my pinkies.

I imagined that when Cynara tested positive on the ovulation prediction kit, we'd load the box into our wobbly-wheeled laundry cart and walk the half-mile to our doctor's office. I would push the cart gallantly over the bumpy brick sidewalk, trying to steer with one hand and hold Cynara's hand with the other. I would gaze into her eyes with the right level of love and romance for this baby-making process, as the jostling of the cart on bricks tattooed the moment on my brain. *This is how we're going to have a baby.*

But that's not how it happened. Cynara ovulated on the weekend, which meant our doctor's office was closed, so we had to strap our box of sperm into a seatbelt and drive across the city to the andrology lab full of silent straight couples, with the men avoiding all eye contact. For us, this was a magical place where babies were made, but for the straight couples, it was a place they were sent to be tested and prodded and given "alternative" options (which to us, sounded like possibility, but to them, sounded like failure). As we waited, we alternately chatted and joked and got teary, while the straight couples stared through the legs of our chairs.

The nurse twisted the top of the metal tank and pulled out a small cylinder that looked like it should contain a core sample of the moon. Inside of that were two tiny vials of hope topped with red plastic caps. She told us some people liked to save them and make earrings out of them. This made perfect sense, so we saved them. We did not question where one would wear these earrings. The nurse thawed one vial and invited us to look at the sperm swimming under a microscope. I looked at the millions of possibilities squiggling under the lens, and nodded like I did at waiters after taking a sip of wine I knew nothing about. *This will do.*

When the nurse left, Cynara changed into her creaky, paper dress. We held hands. The nurse returned with a small, needleless syringe, attached to a long tube that she guided into Cynara's uterus. She handed me the syringe. I looked into Cynara's eyes, the fluorescent lights dimmed, and everything outside of our tightly tethered web faded away as I slowly pushed plunger. *This is how we're going to have a baby.* They gave us fifteen minutes alone for Cynara to keep her hips elevated. I shut the door and took a picture of her with her knee-high rainbow socks silhouetted against the pocked drop-ceiling tiles. I turned out the lights, played "Lucky Star" on her phone, and held it up to her uterus. We held hands and sang along as the world went blurry, and I pictured a sperm swimming to the beat of Madonna, wiggling its way into a Cynara-shaped egg.

For several years, our calendars were graffitied with multicoloured notes: my periods, Cynara's periods, ovulations, and weeks' worth of appointments that we had to make and then cancel one by one until that blue strip or smiley face told us to keep the appointment and call in sick. Luckily, I was still an assistant teacher, so I didn't have to make a substitute plan each time I called in sick. At first, we would pee on pink plastic sticks with cute digital smiley faces. Later, it was the budget sticks with just stripes. By the end, it was simply strips of paper that barely changed colour, which arrived in giant Ziploc bags from India.

Once, when it was my turn to lie on my back wearing the crunchy paper dress, we had a new nurse who left the door open and shouted, "Come see them swimming!" to anyone passing by. She fiddled with three sets of glasses tangled in chains around her neck and nested in her hair. Cynara later named her "Fretterazine"—fake Italian for "one who frets." Fretterazine focused the microscope so passionately that the lens broke the slide in two and became covered in anonymous-but-willing-to-be-known-at-age-eighteen sperm (which costs over a hundred dollars more). "Where'd you put the form?" she asked as she rifled around the room in a circle and then flipped up my paper dress as if she might have misplaced the consent form inside my vagina. I looked at Cynara, wondering if we were getting the right sperm, or if she might be injecting me with some old mayonnaise from the door of the staff fridge.

I'd never been invested in getting pregnant myself. But still, once I started trying, each period sunk me lower. I'd have an extra beer, or two, or sometimes a cigarette that I'd quit many years before, even though I had cut out caffeine and nonorganic fruit to make this baby a sickeningly pure nest. I thought back to the organic sadness of those couples in our adoption class and felt irrationally hopeless that I'd failed at something so primal.

DIY

It is surprisingly easy to do this at home. You buy needleless syringes, like the kind you use for giving medicine to kids. You think of every ex, old gay BFF, close friend, other person's family member, or mild acquaintance who would be willing to have a relationship with your kid but not be too invested. You rule them out when they are dying to have kids of their own or when they ask, "Do I get the kid if you both die?" You invite them over, chat nervously as your wife pulls down all the blinds, as if they might need the run of the entire house. Then you walk your dog and try not to think about the details of the event taking place in your bathroom. When you come back, you try to find the balance between being polite to this person who is giving you most important gift you could ever imagine, and rushing them out as you picture each sperm dying one by one. When they leave, you fill the small syringe and put it in your wife, or she puts it in you at home in your own bed, where you are free to keep your legs in the air for an hour and indulge in superstitions of your own making.

After the margins of our credit cards wore thin and we had exhausted our rolodex of potential known-donors, we moved beyond friends of friends, and someone who knew someone from work, until we found ourselves at a Panera in one of those suburbs perched on the first highway loop around the city. We were here to meet a donor. In the parking lot, I unconsciously memorized the patterns of cars and spaces and rainbows of oil. On the sidewalk, a stream of granular, iridescent, blue slushy, dammed with sopped up lottery tickets and cigarette butts snaked towards some yet-to-be-determined lowest point. *This is how we're going to have a baby.*

Cynara and I worked out a code; if either of us didn't like him, as we were eating we would suddenly say, "I should have gotten the cookie!" (Panera was running a special where you could add a cookie onto your order for ninety-nine cents.)

As we waited in line, my mind slid down his face, with nothing to grab on to. He started rocking back and forth. I do that when I'm nervous: shift my weight from one leg to the other when I have no props to hold or pockets to put my hands in. He kept rocking—not just shifting weight but keeping time like a metronome. I looked at the cookie. I looked at Cynara. But her eyes were sparkling at something not visible to me. Then again, she was always sparkling. I saw a documentary once, about how we're all drawn to each other based on the smell of pheromones from people who have immunities we don't have. Maybe pheromones were conspiring to make us an extremely healthy baby. Or maybe she was just being nice, like she is to everyone—and it's not even a show because she actually likes most people, which is something I admire about her and find completely incomprehensible.

Halfway through our soups and sandwiches, we knew he was gay-but-closeted, living in his mother's basement, and only lit up when he talked about the detective show *Castle*. I imagined taking a healthy, mystery-loving toddler to visit their donor in the basement, watching them rock back and forth, in sync, sharing something they didn't share with me.

When we ran out of things to say, he pulled out a home HIV test and started clawing at the plastic wrap. He offered, "I can prick my finger in front of you, right here at the table!" I looked around for a Board of Health sign that could help us out of this situation and saw Cynara's smile waiver like heat coming off the road. It wasn't until we walked across the parking lot, got in the car, and safely shut the door that we both said, "I should've gotten the cookie."

Babies

I can't tell you all the details of where our babies actually came from because, as Cynara reminded me, these details are now their stories. Every week, old ladies bless our cart full of kids in the supermarket and ask where they got those blue eyes. Depending on how rushed we are, we'll say "the donor," or "my father," or "I have no idea; it could have been anyone!"

In the end, there were some miracles—kind and generous donors, state health insurance kicking into high gear for our "advanced maternal age," subsidized medical methods so effective that we ended up with twins, and courthouses full of judges snuggling our babies and posing for pictures after they pronounced them all legally ours. Our family has grown to include more people than I ever could have imagined. Like in all families, some members are wonderful and some are bat-shit crazy, but we try to keep all the doors ajar because we can't predict who will be important to our kids in the future.

I *can* tell you that there was one month we were desperate enough to gamble. We both inseminated. I was nervous.

"Just watch, this is the time it will work."

"Great!" Cynara said. "That's the idea. Like lighting a cigarette to make the bus come."

Cynara is the Ernie to my Bert, the Frog to my Toad.

"But what if they both work?" I asked.

"Then we'll have lesbian twins! Like Irish twins but even closer."

"But who will buy the pickles and ice cream? Who'll drive us to the hospital?"

And that was how Cynara got pregnant.

Thankfully, we weren't both pregnant, but I wasn't sure how to hold all that happiness and sadness at the same time—like a sponge so full any touch would make me spill. But there was no time for that. I would be the ridiculous breathing coach (that our teacher admitted was made up to keep the coach busy). I would practice driving the back route to the hospital, memorizing where the potholes were to avoid. People congratulated both of us and threw showers for both of us. I came out to my first-grade students, the last people in my life who didn't know this about me. They drew me pictures, made me cards, and put their baby-name suggestions in a jar.

I read all the books about pregnancy that compare your fetus to various fruits and paid close attention to the "Dad Tips" (e.g., try to help clean up once in a while). I also read anything I could find about queer nonbiological parents and joined online groups that jangled my alarmist nerves. Late at night, Cynara snored next to me as I read confessions that orbited around flesh, milk, jealousy, and resentment. I didn't think I would feel those things, but how would I know?

I became a parent when Cynara gave birth. It was fast and crazy, and she did not take any drugs. She told me the baby was coming, and I got our vegan wraps to go. I drove the back way to the hospital. I brought the red backpack full of Yahtzee, a head scratcher, books, and movies we would never open. I left the car running with the doors open (the way they said it would never happen) and checked her in, afraid that when I went to park I would miss the baby.

We had practiced holding ice until it hurt, bouncing on exercise balls, and getting into all kinds of woman-friendly poses that would help the baby come out. She didn't use any of them. She had joked about screaming "This is all your fault!" at me, like they do in sitcoms, but there was no time between contractions for jokes. The doctor told me to direct her energy down instead of out, and I said I was not about to tell my wife to stop yelling at this particular moment.

When Julia was born, they put her on Cynara's chest, and she held her with stunned love. A nurse took a picture with a pink hospital camera with big pixels. When I cut the cord, it felt like cutting something alive, but it didn't make me squeamish the way I thought it would. Then they wrapped Julia up and put her in my arms, and my cells tingled, and I could not tell where the edges of my body, the blanket, and Julia were. I still feel like that when I hug her. We took turns holding her and staring at her for hours. We had read all the books, but we didn't actually understand that she would never sleep.

When we got home, Julia cried when we put her down. So we took turns. I would sit back on the couch with her spread out like a frog on my chest until I heard her breathing change. I would watch her and then read, while drinking seltzer, trying to stay awake, and feeling so lucky that I got to be her mom. The stars and the laws and the sperm and the eggs had finally lined up in such a way to make this rarest of constellations and perfect baby possible.

Julia cried for about four months straight. I would "shhh" her, rock her, and rub her belly, and, finally, Cynara would nurse her. I started to wonder if there was something about that fleshy bonding that I had underestimated.

When other people held her and she cried, they would hand her to Cynara. Despite my brain's reassurance, my heart still flooded with cold water. But Cynara would say, "Give her to Stacy." When people asked, "Who's the mom?" Cynara would say, "We both are," before I had to say it with that edge I could never completely iron out of my voice. And when, even at home, I felt like I couldn't comfort her more than any stranger, Cynara left me alone with her and encouraged me to go to singalongs and playgroups without her until Julia and I made our own memories and rituals.

My pregnancy was different; it was full of needles, regularly scheduled events, and drugs, which suited me (minus the needles). We went to a lab that looked like a hotel where there were needles to test levels, make things grow, take things out, and put things in. At home, Cynara watched YouTube videos to show her how to give me shots every night. I drove over the bridge each day as the sun glowed pink and orange over the city to get my blood tested before work. The numbers were high. There were two of them in there, the nurse told us with absolutely no inflection. It was Cynara's turn to tear up with joy, while I was temporarily too stunned to feel. The birth was scheduled like a haircut. Cynara held my hand and kept talking to distract me from the fact that I was being sawed down the middle like a magician's assistant. They wiped, weighed, and wrapped the babies and handed them to Cynara, who brought them to my face one by one.

Cynara had pumped breastmilk for months so she could nurse them too. We took turns with the double My Brest Friend pillow. I was surprised that when the boundaries of my body were filled, then stretched, and finally porous, I was not bothered. It felt surprisingly warm to be uncontained with Lea and Zoe latched like a litter of kittens, but I was still happy I didn't have to do it by myself. Julia wanted to hold them right away, so when we got home we surrounded her with pyramids of stunt-man pillows and propped the babies on her lap as she shuddered with joy.

Giving birth did not make me feel like more of a "real mom," but it did help me see that all of our kids cry for "Other-Mommy" when one of us asks them to eat, pee, get in a car seat, or try to foil any of their gloriously free-willed plans. These momentary shifts are only dependent on biology in the sense that they're based on how much recent time we've spent together and who's eaten, pooped, or slept enough (adults included).

Like most parents, I think my children are perfect. It's something I try not to say out loud because there's nothing more annoying than someone posting a thousand nearly identical pictures of their kids online or complaining about driving to too many state championships. But this is not what I mean. I mean my children are absolutely perfect, with their shimmering joy they can't contain in their solid bodies, the shyness that makes them refuse to speak to kids of adults I want to be friends with, and the rolling tantrums they have on the most bacteria-ridden public bathroom floors. My heart glows warm and expands, vibrating molecules that tingle out the top of my head until we are all one mixed-up golden ball of love.

In the end, we had slightly more children than we had planned— and some extra embryos in storage. After a year, the fertility center asked us to make a decision. The only checkboxes on the form were: ☐ annual storage fee, ☐ research, or ☐ destruction.

I was leaning towards research, but Cynara is a much better person than I am. She walks dogs for people living with HIV, secretly shovels snowy sidewalks for elderly neighbours in the middle of the night, and drives grandmas and grandchildren home from bus stops. She also has more vision. So she asked, "Shouldn't we donate these to someone?" It never would have occurred to me that we could go beyond our legally contracted options. When Cynara was pregnant she said, "After all this, I'd love to help someone else have a baby ... if my last egg weren't limping down my fallopian tubes with a cane." But, now, we actually had something to give.

As always, Cynara figured out the logistics. She found a lawyer and created our pixelated profile, weeding out the people on a mission from God to save every embryo. She found Maureen, a single woman about our age, who was interested in having contact with the embryo donors and their families. On a work trip to Boston, she stopped by our house. She was warm, relaxed, and not a fraction as desperate as I'd been in a similar situation. We chatted easily as our dog barked and our three-year-old and one-year-old twins swirled around her. Despite the pressure, it felt like we already knew her. The first two embryos didn't work out, but the third one stuck.

When Maureen's baby was almost one, we took the train to meet at a halfway point in an industrial city full of crumbing, once-grand buildings. When we met in the hotel lobby, Julia shouted, "Baby Rosie!" and ran to pick her up. Lea scurried behind her with her small Flintstone steps, and Zoe skipped behind with her big skips. They all hugged Rosie, and she smiled at me. The symmetry was shocking. A soft geometry reflected through all of them and fit perfectly into some rounded grooves in my heart. Something fizzed, bubbled.

The wind was so painfully cold that it ripped the breath out of our lungs and made all of our children cry. We spent the weekend braving the one block between the two hotels and shivering in the hotel pool until the kids had what they called "fwinkles" on their fingers. Our kids took turns holding Rosie and crawling with her in the lobby. They sang songs and yelped when she laughed or briefly stood. Despite only seeing the insides of two hotels and one grocery store, our kids declared, "This is the best trip ever!"

I used to love a heartbreaking train station goodbye—the kind where you had mixed up your heart with someone willy-nilly, so when the train pulled away, bits of your heart stretched thin and tore as the wheels chugged faster and faster towards a vanishing point. But this was different. We hugged Maureen and Rosie and helped them onto the train as snowflakes swirled. When train pulled away, it tugged on my heart but did not rip it. I felt my heart expanding steadily, like the universe, still radiating out from that first Big-Bang kiss with Cynara.

Endnotes

1. Abbreviations stand for: trying to conceive, the two-week wait, intrauterine insemination, known donors, willing-to-be-known, and in vitro fertilization.

Chapter Thirteen

"Are You Having the Next One?"Or, How I Learned to Stop Worrying and Love My (Empty) Womb

Patricia Curmi

I t started early, when our now almost three-year-old was still in her (other) mama's womb. When we announced to people that we were expecting and my partner was carrying, their eyes would shoot from her not-yet-bulging belly to me and say in a friendly way: "Congratulations! Are you having the next one?" Or they would ask variations of that same question: "Will it be your turn next?" or "Are you going to have one each?" "I...We..." I stuttered in response, despite having rehearsed this in my head while cycling or in the shower. I finally said, "No, I think [my partner] makes great babies, so we're sticking with her womb!" Sometimes, I would jokingly add: "I like to outsource the difficult bit." Much kicking of self was done in the moments that followed. Coward, I would tell myself. Why didn't you push back and act like the fierce rad queer that you pretend to be when anyone with a slightly asymmetrical haircut comes within ten metres of you?

It niggled me then, it stung just after our baby was born, and it annoys me now, after three years of parenting of an actual human toddler. I am sure people will eventually stop asking me this question. But I want to explore here why I switched from expecting to carry our second one to again being the nongestational parent and how I understood and reacted to this line of questioning during pregnancy, birth, the early months, and now with a toddler. I also want to flip this question around a bit and try and understand why it bothers me and what people are getting at, even subconsciously, when they ask it.

I am grateful to quickly add that this issue is possibly the only specific difference I've encountered as a nongestational, nonbiological parent in a lesbian couple. I wish all nontraditional families could experience the legal and social support we have. Not a week goes by where I don't thank my queer, feminist, and union-repping ancestors and siblings for their struggle for me to be able to sleep next to our newborn and partner in the hospital; to sign my name on the birth certificate; to live without fear of a brick being thrown through our window or finding hateful graffiti on our door; and to have paid parental leave and flexible working without discrimination, among many other things. Sometimes, I thank them silently, in my head, and then sometimes I email them while crying and listening to the *Shortbus* soundtrack. Sleep deprivation is a real thing, and you only realize that when you're googling "Peter Tatchell[1] email address" at 3:00 a.m. while pinned down by a snoring baby.

We live on the south coast in the United Kingdom (UK), in a small but hugely hippy, liberal city. We moved there when our kid was one from the large and mostly liberal capital, London. I'm white and British; my partner is Mexican. She occasionally gets the racist and xenophobic "go back to your country" comments or has to endure stereotypes about Mexicans. In the past, we've also occasionally had homophobic comments shouted at us (the most common one is a scream of "Lesbian!"—so factual I have no retort); I've also been chased down the street by a guy who got angry when I suggested maybe his abusive language towards me and my partner holding hands was due to his own repressed homosexual desires and that he should find a man willing to experiment with him. But I'd have to say our experience hasn't been typical of what I know to be the more challenging, or life-threatening, experience of so many queers, both in the UK and other countries, including our own loved ones. I'm sharing this right up front because I think I'm about as close as possible to the life queer people—and in the case of my partner, queer people of colour—deserve to be living.

In fact, one of the issues I have experienced as a queer parent, linked to the titular question of "are you going next?," is that since becoming a parent, the queerness seems to be fading as part of my identity, as I am absorbed into the mostly mainstream 'hood of parents, specifically motherhood. In so many ways, I realize that this is a comparably great problem to have.

In the early days of donor searching, when we had not yet conceived, I went to the bookshop to find something on queer conception and parenting. I know now that there are some great resources out there in print and online, but, at the time, it was my first foray into the subject. I walked over to the pregnancy and parenting section and saw the shelves bulging with all kinds of books on the topic, but nothing from an LGBT angle. Thinking I must have been categorizing it wrongly, I trundled over to the LGBT section to see what was there. Great stuff, familiar stuff, but no parenting stuff. Since our kid was born, I feel I have been wandering between those two aisles, not yet sure how to be in both of them at the same time.

Back when I was firmly hanging out in the queer section of the store (in reality, I don't hang out that much in bookshops at all), my partner of six years and I decided to make a family. At first, we considered adoption, but because we lived in a communal house and we weren't willing to give that up, adoption wasn't an option for us in our borough. We had a vision of living in a queer family commune (which, as an aside, wilted away after our kid's arrival). So we turned to baby making in the old fashioned-ish way: home insemination with a known donor.

Before I had ever met my partner or thought seriously about starting a family, I had always imagined that I would either adopt, or carry, any kids I would parent. I liked the idea of being pregnant, breastfeeding, and caring fulltime for kids. I can't say what breeze this idea wafted in on, or how it planted itself in my head, but it laid the root in the back of my brain, and by the time I got to the discussion about having kids, it had put out little shoots.

In contrast, my partner did not want to have kids when we met. She did not see that in her life plan. She definitely did not see herself getting pregnant or identify as a mother. She did not idealize the breastfeeding relationship or looking after a newborn or toddler. If anything, she could vaguely imagine relating to an older child but in the kind of benevolent, uninvolved way of sitcom fathers from the 1960s. She would make sandwiches but not braid hair, fix things in the house but not deal with tantrums.

Yet one year and nine months later, my partner was sitting in our house breastfeeding our new baby she'd birthed while I was heading back to work.

Why did my partner carry our first child and not me? Two big reasons and one smaller one. First, we're a bicultural couple. My partner is part of a very small Mexican diaspora in the UK. She grew up in a big Mexican city with tortas ahogadas, mariachi, piñatas (but proper ones, she insists, where you had to fight over the sweets), fiestas, Juan Gabriel power ballads, and all the vibrant, energizing aspects of a childhood and adolescence in Mexico. She isn't blind to the country's complex social and political issues, but let's just say she starts weeping with nostalgia exactly ten seconds into a one-minute cheesy tourist advert for Mexico that shows the country's cultural and scenic highlights. So how could she convey to our future child what it means to be Mexican if we were living in the UK surrounded by British culture, with the other parent being British? For her, having a child with the same genetic coding was a substitute for having a child with the same cultural coding. Clearly, they are different things, but at the time the decision was made, her worry was being the "other" in our own family.

For myself, having lived with a friend and her kid previously and having spent time with children in various capacities, I was confident that genes would not be a big stumbling block for me. I felt no strong associations with my own mixed genetic heritage and knew my family (those I still spoke to) would not have an issue with whether my child had our familial DNA.

The second main reason was age. Although we only differed in age by a couple of years (only eighteen months, she points out), we felt that the older partner trying first would be working along the grain of biology, instead of against it.

The third reason, and at the time a more distant assumption, was that I would, indeed, carry a second child. I could wait, I thought, because this child will be my child, and I'll have the experience of carrying and birthing the next one.

So, we found a donor, wrote a contract, and experienced much joy. It only took one try at insemination, and my partner was pregnant. There was much shock, even with a planned pregnancy. I pretty much continued on in my role as research gatherer. I imagine my cave-dwelling, queer-expecting ancestors shunning the more instinctive and thrill-seeking hunter-gathers, to join around the fire to overthink baby slings and obsess over nightlights that didn't attract the sabre tooth tigers. If Google had existed then, they might have typed, as I did at some point in those nine months, "Can loud noise make a fetus go deaf?" They might have asked "How soft does cheese have to be before it's dangerous in pregnancy?" or "Can a fetus get depressed if they hear sad music?"

The point is that I had a role. I didn't have the big belly or feel the kicks. But I sung to the baby-to-be, found romper suits with Dolly Parton lyrics, made blankets, wrote letters, massaged my partner, and visualized this little being in our lives. I'm not sure what difference it made, but my partner didn't exactly thrive on the attention of being pregnant. I ask her now if she played it down to make sure I didn't feel excluded, but she maintains that she just didn't love losing her body autonomy and feeling so heavy.

I can honestly say I didn't feel any resentment towards my partner about her being pregnant and not me. The only place I'd say insecurity popped up was in the nomenclature of parenthood. My partner, though definitely not feeling like a mother, as she interpreted it, decided to call herself "mamá." It was a nod to her being Mexican. I prevaricated and couldn't decide whether I was a mummy or something else. I didn't reflect much on my reaction to names at the time, but I now realize there was a definite worry, connected to embarrassment and shame, that I was faking it to be staking a claim on the (sacred!) title of "mum" and that I had somehow snuck through a shortcut into motherhood, without having to carry or birth this yet-to-be born baby. It felt, too, exposing, too much like I was pretending to be something that I wasn't sure I was. At that point, I had nothing but neurotic Google searches to admit me into the motherhood club. I remember looking on online parenting forums thinking I'd be laughed out if I revealed I was with someone who was pregnant but had no genetic connection to the baby. "Am I really that different to a nanny?" I would ask myself in harsher moments. And this kid will have their other genetic parent—the donor—in our lives, although they would not be parenting them or be responsible for them in any way.

I settled on a made-up name for myself by merging and shortening "mom" and "homo" to "Momo." (It started as a joke and just stuck.) I love this name now, and I get a warm loving feeling when I hear our toddler say it. It's our special name. She also now calls me Mummy as well, and I don't have the same reservations about the title as when she hadn't yet been born; I feel entitled to be her parent after three years of 24/7 parenting.

And that was why the question about "going next" didn't feel totally alienating when it was asked while we were expecting our first child: I hadn't even gone this time! I had no idea what it meant to jump into parenthood and how totally it would knock my centre of gravity and leave me freefalling into love and euphoria and worry and tiredness and all the rest. More than anything, it just added to the background hum of my own worry that I would not really be a parent, and the kid would know it.

Our oldest was born by C-section, and it was, to date, the most epic and disorienting moment in my life. I was the first person to see her little face, and I put my hand on her, spoke to her, and then carried her over to see my partner. My heart felt so full. Within hours of cradling her little body (we got a bit delirious and decided skin to skin meant we couldn't put her down, even for a second), a nurse asked us the fateful question, which was the first time I'd heard it post-baby. After telling my partner "Not to worry, you can try for a natural birth next time," the nurse swiveled round, laughed, and said "But I suppose you'll want to go next!" Haha, hoho, hehe. In one swipe, she knocked the birth experience of my partner and, I felt, insinuated that I had not just been part of the incredible experience of bringing our daughter into the world. As so often would be the case, my response was a weak smile while internally making excuses about knowing what she really meant. The question had already started to bother me a little bit more than when the baby was hypothetical or in utero.

Over the first three months of the baby's life, people could have asked me what I had for breakfast and I would have told them, lip wobbling and on the verge of tears, that I ate some nondescript food looking into the eyes of the most amazing baby. It was an emotional time. And no sleep, did I mention we didn't sleep much?

This was a period when the "going next" line of questions came thick and fast. I came to know it as the "everybody needs to comment about something" phase, and since the baby didn't do much other than lie there and look perfect, they turned their commentary to other things, like what style of parenting we did (we call it "chaotic"); were we sleeping much (why would you ask that?!); and would my womb be performing the miracle act of creating life for our family when we chose to expand it (weak smile, internal frown).

In the first three months postbirth, while my partner breastfed and did an amazing job nourishing our baby, I focused on the research gathering, the nappy changing, and the soothing, as I didn't smell like breast/chest milk. Although I had successfully induced lactation prior to her birth, I decided in the final phase of pregnancy that, along with having a different name, I would embrace a different role to mother. Breast/chest feeding felt too intimate an act for me—the mother-by-research—to intrude on. People would think I was weird for putting my breast in the mouth of a baby that didn't share my genes or I didn't grow inside me. I know, I know, it seems ridiculous now, but that's how insecurities work, I suppose. I'm happy with my decision, now, for other reasons but not so happy with my discomfort about breastfeeding and the thought processes that fed into the decision.

This newborn phase was the hardest time, emotionally, for me to hear the question. I had just gone through this tumultuous life change; everything had changed, but most things looked the same, and I had no idea yet how things would land. I didn't have more than a caretaking role with the baby because they mainly needed their physical needs to be met. I did it in loving ways, and loved talking to her and massaging her after baths and all the loving stuff, but there were moments where I was so unsure whether I was adding much to this baby's life.

I can clearly remember taking our then-five-month-old to baby yoga and some of the women doing the class chatting to me and saying, "Oh, your body is doing well postpartum." Forgetting my self-image, which took it as a blow that it seemed credible I was recovering from carrying a baby inside it, I faced the awkward moment of not only coming out but also coming out as a nonbirthing mum.

With the instability of this time, people's questions about whether I would have another baby down the line really hurt. They fed into my worry that I somehow wasn't getting it right and would never be a real mum. The baby cried for her real mum and wanted her real mum's milk; and the smell of her real mum was something I felt as a blow when I couldn't soothe that screaming infant. And then I felt a wave of guilt and disloyalty to the tiny being I loved so immeasurably: Did I want a baby that belonged to me, that would need me so I would feel needed? Was I that narcissistic? How could I already be failing this baby by thinking about the next one, whom I'd be better able to comfort and who might not grow up to think I was a fake? I had wanted to go next after all. I chastised myself. I was making it about me and not putting our daughter's needs first.

I'm not painting this time as a dark one. Truly it was a period I think back to as full of deep, delightful connection with my partner and baby. The self-doubting thoughts, like the well-intentioned questions, happened suddenly, like skin caught in a zip. But they were often forgotten quickly in the day-to-day whirlwind of life adjusting to a new baby.

It's only now, with an opinion-holding, will-expressing three-year-old, that I can look back and reflect on what it meant to be that new nongestational parent to a baby that is a person but does not express personhood in any verbal or intellectual way. I realize how many of my wounds from people asking that question came not from their glancing blows but from my own internal jabs that reinforced them as confirming what I saw coming: This kid will not think I am her mum. Nobody else will see me as her mum because she already has one with a stronger claim. Of course, that isn't what friends, family and strangers had in mind when they asked me about going next, but it held a mirror up to the fear I felt.

I now have a deeper understanding that parent—a mum or dad or whatever—isn't a noun; it's a verb. I parent every day, and in the doing, I have become. I don't want to sound too cheesy, but just as we delivered her to her first breath, our daughter delivered us into parenthood. She taught us how to parent her.

And we have a bond that feels to me healthy and full of love. I don't look to our daughter to meet my need to be needed. I don't look to her for reassurance of what I mean to her. And she varies who she wants to meet different needs at different times. That feels right. In fact, when she chose her other mother to change her nappy, it felt very right.

It hurts less to hear the question at this stage, but it annoys me more, if that makes sense. I see it for what it is, and I read less into it. I want the person to know that I had this kid; there is no next that I will have more than this one. Sure, I get what they're saying. The next one will exit via my vagina or lower abdomen and have my facial features. But that is called birth and being genetically related. And their question implies that my nonbirthed and nonrelated kid is somehow a trial run, or that I must surely long to have a biologically related and birthed baby.

I want to ask them whether they would you ask someone who had adopted whether they were going to keep trying for a biological kid. On reflection, this is probably exactly what adoptive parents go through and, thus, reinforces the point about society perceiving real motherhood being connected to genetics and vaginas.

And that's the issue. The question tells me a lot about how we as society see pregnancy as a rite of passage for women while undervaluing the act of parenting and the nonbirth parent's role, usually a father. There are also the "leaving a legacy" and "bloodline" issues that manifest in any assumption that I must be longing to carry a baby that I share DNA with.

So I weakly smiled my way through the questions in the early months and swatted the question away by the early years. And, then, because we hit that sweet spot when our toddler seemed super cool, we reasoned the following "We're sleeping again, our furniture is no longer covered in breast/chest milk, and our kid is lovely. And was it really that bad the first time with a newborn? Shall we have a sibling and a squidgy baby that will become like aforementioned awesome kid?" (Note: The window of "cool toddler" lasted exactly from the moment of our decision to the moment of conception for us.)

By the time we got to this discussion, I had already formed my opinion: I didn't want to carry our second child. I didn't want to have a genetically related second child. It felt like something firm and true and solid in my brain. By carrying the next one, I'd be validating the go-nexters. Yes, they now had a name.

I'll start with the odd and sometimes ugly reasons I wrestled with to reach this decision. And then I'll highlight the reasons that are borne out of love of what we have rather than a fear of what we don't. But I'll air the uglier reasons, just because I think it's important to share the hidden iceberg of dark emotions and prejudices that "Are you going next?" raises for me.

First is the protection of my relationship with our eldest daughter, which expressed itself as fear of favouritism. I have been lucky enough to be part of a couple of brilliant online groups for queer parents, so I know that having different genetic and birthing relationships with each kid doesn't have to pose much of a threat to anyone's relationship with anyone, and that over time, it can disappear as a factor anyway. As one great lesbian blogger who had birthed one child while her partner birthed the other with the same donor put it: "We're related in a line, each connected biologically to the person next to them." I think that's a beautiful way to see it.

Although biology can create a preference and an emotional connection, my fear was rooted in a deeper, more personal memory of a parent consistently favouring one child (though it changed who was the favourite) and playing each of my siblings and myself off against each other in pursuit for that parental love. I heard the distant yet familiar drum of worry: Will either child think we are favouring the child we birthed? Once it dawned on me that this was lurking in the unprocessed childhood issues department of my mind, it was easier to face and see it as something we could overcome, especially since I've seen firsthand other families doing it. But I'd be lying if I said this didn't emerge early on as a worry.

Connected to the favouritism issue, for me, was accepting that no child will have the same relationship with both parents and that relationships will change over time regardless. In trying to recreate the brilliant bond I have with our eldest with the second born, I realized I was already doing the thing that would be my undoing: comparing the kids instead of taking them each as entirely their own individuals.

And while I'm sharing embarrassing hang-ups I wish I didn't have to share but will anyway, another one is the need for my children to be genetically related to each other. This may sound unusual for someone who genuinely didn't have much hesitation about not being genetically related to their kids. I didn't realize I had a hidden prejudice of half-siblings that lingered from, who knows, talk shows and stories about women with lots of kids from different dads until it popped up when contemplating having the second child. On an intellectual level, in all my life's experience, I know this to be wrong on every level. I know people who have different mothers and the same father, the same father and a different mother, and I know sibling relationships are mostly a result of personality and family dynamic and of time spent together and parental treatment—not because 50 per cent of their genes are from the same source or not.

I knew this, and yet. Throw in a healthy dose of worry that I was already giving our kids a different kind of family and add a fear rooted in internalized homophobia that told me I'm already being selfish by trying to have the family I want, despite going against nature to make it and raise it. It was a surprising stumbling block and one I was—and still am—ashamed to talk about. It took me a while to get to the point where this wasn't an issue anymore. The residual echo of this now-extinct concern is the desire for the kids to be best able to relate and support each other in their experience of being donor-conceived children in a queer family. It lurks as a spectre, still connected to that guilt of leading them into an alternative family, and then stranding them with no peer who has the same experience—as if two siblings from a traditional family even have the same experience anyway!

This fear's more realistic aspect stems from my partner's cultural and ethnic heritage. It remains as present for the second child as it did for the first. We wondered what it might mean for one kid to identify with Mexico and Latino as an ethnic heritage, whereas the other didn't, considering the country and the culture were going to be an important presence in our lives.

And before even getting to any of the parenting stuff, I had the irrational worry that I would not conceive the first time and my pregnancy would not go as smoothly as my partner's. I love my body, for all its wonky rebelliousness, but the thought of trying and failing to get pregnant month after month while we knew my partner got pregnant after one try made me feel like I was already under pressure to perform.

When I write these reasons down, their potency seems to melt away. Each one of them has valid counterarguments; each one focuses on a worry of what-if, a skittishness of what may lurk in the shadows rather than a faith in the love and strength of our family and supportive community. So, I'll end with the final thing that convinced me that I would not carry our second child: I am good at being a momo who grows babies in the warmth of my unconditional love and not my womb. I am good at being a conception-, pregnancy-, and birth-support person. I am good at knowing what a momo does and showing our newfound, mostly straight, parenting community that the person who doesn't birth the babies can be fully active in their life. It's not a source of regret for me but one of immense joy. I have made the role my own, even though I didn't envision being a nongestational parent. I've discovered that I enjoy my relationship with our daughter not being rooted in shared genetic traits. It has challenged me to keep seeing and reseeing her as a person wholly unto herself, free from my projections and expectations of what a child with my genes should be like.

For the moment, I'm bracing myself for the next evolution of the question after two children have joined our family: "Did you not want to have any?" or, perhaps, "Did you not want a turn?" or "Can you not have any?" But maybe I'm being cynical. I hope I'll have a better answer than a weak smile next time.

Endnotes

1. A human rights activist who led the way for LGBT rights in the UK and Europe and an incredible person.

Chapter Fourteen

No, That's Mom

Allie Robbins

"No, That's Mom."

That's what my two-year-old says when I pick him up from daycare and someone tells him that his Mama or Mommy has arrived. For most kids, mom, mama, mommy, and mother can be used interchangeably. For my son, there is a big difference between Mama and Mom. Mama is his biological mother, my wife. I am Henry's Mom. So, when his friend points at me and exclaims "Henry's Mama!" my son feels the need to firmly correct him.

When my son was around two and-a half years old, my wife and I went to a Brandi Carlile concert. Brandi Carlile was already special to us because her song "The Story" was our wedding song. Yet as good musicians always seem to do, Brandi Carlile continues to have the perfect words to capture important moments in my life, far beyond my wedding. Before singing her song "The Mother" about her experience as a nonbiological mother, Brandi talked about the difficulty, and importance, of figuring out your place as the nonbiological mother.[1] Heterosexual people often try to place nonbiological moms in the role of father because it's what they can relate to. But that's not who we are. Although each person and each relationship are obviously different, it's up to us to carve out a space to be our true selves and to continue to pave the way for the normalization of various family structures. The more visibly same-sex families can claim their place in the world, the more open others will be to seeing that there are many ways to parent and many ways to be a family. My journey so far has often meant battling heteronormative stereotypes, sometimes struggling for visibility, fighting my own insecurities, and falling in love with all of the challenges and joys of being a mother.

People say that motherhood changes everything. They're right. When I went back to work a few weeks after Henry was born, I remember wondering how everyone around me was functioning. Most of my coworkers have children, yet they didn't seem to be obsessing about them every minute. They were able to get their work done and seemed, at least, to act like they thought the work they were doing mattered to them. In contrast, I was completely consumed with thoughts of my new baby boy, and every second away from him was excruciating. I truly couldn't understand how people managed to live their lives when their hearts were miles away inside of their children. As Henry has gotten older, I have been better able to function at work, but the importance of everything else in life has definitely diminished.

The first part of our journey was figuring out how to make us Mama and Mom. For a variety of reasons, we chose the route of using intrauterine insemination to impregnate my wife with the sperm of an anonymous donor. We spent months researching the process and reviewing profiles of potential sperm donors, as if we were engaged in extreme online dating. We decided we wanted the donor to share some of my ethnic makeup, since my wife would be carrying. We signed up for multiple sperm banks, made spreadsheets of donors we liked, compared them to each other, showed the finalists to our friends, and, finally, decided on a donor that we thought would be a good fit. Of course, we think we made the right choice because Henry is brilliant and gorgeous, but the process is scary. We are constantly reading stories of people suing sperm banks for doing a poor job of vetting their donors or sending women the wrong sperm. The list of worries is seemingly endless. Is this guy really who he says he is? What if there are health issues in his family that pop up? How will we know about them? Will Henry really be able to get in touch with him when he turns eighteen? We opted for the type of donor relationship that allows our son to reach out to the sperm bank, and the sperm bank will then contact the donor. If the sperm bank succeeds in making contact and if the donor still agrees, Henry can meet his donor. This is a wonderful and terrifying prospect that I am sure I will have a lot of uneasy feelings about when the time comes.

Once my wife got pregnant, there was the birthing class. We were the only nonheterosexual couple. Our teacher was very conscious of using gender-neutral language, and, overall, we had a fairly inclusive experience. But my certificate at the end still said father, and everything was divided by sex, which was just enough to remind me every minute or two that I was different. To be fair, I did literally sign up for that, as the class we took was The Bradley Method for Husband-Coached Natural Childbirth. Yet even when you sign up for something like that—knowing you will be the only one of your kind, knowing you will be different—it still never feels good. You feel invisible and in the spotlight all at once. It just puts you a little bit on edge (as if the idea that you had to coach your wife through childbirth and would then be a parent wasn't already anxiety-inducing enough).

Our birth story began on a warm August morning. I awoke at 5:13 a.m. to my wife saying "My water just broke!" I jolted up and responded, "Oh... okay!" I called the doctor, and we ran around grabbing a few last-minute things for the hospital. My superhero wife drove herself to the hospital while having contractions because I don't like to drive and she didn't want to deal with my anxiety. A few hours later, my wife had a C-section. Our son was frank breech, which means that his bottom was facing the birth canal instead of his head, making a vaginal delivery dangerous. His stubbornness—as demonstrated in his desire to stick his butt out—as well as his immunity to the danger posed by the position and height of his body in relation to the ground would return in full force as a two-year-old.

After cleaning him up, a nurse handed me this hairy, red, swollen baby, and told me to wait in recovery while they cleaned up my wife. "Wait, you're going to leave me alone with him?" I thought. "I have never even changed a diaper. I don't know how to take care of him." But, in my usual silent way, I took the baby, followed orders, and sat down waiting for my wife to be wheeled into the recovery room, desperately hoping that someone would check on us to relieve me of the sole responsibility for caring for this new life. So, it began: my journey of being a completely unprepared mom to an incredible boy. After what felt like an eternity, my wife was wheeled into the room. We placed Henry in her arms; he manoeuvered up to her breast and began to drink. From the moment they first touched each other, they have had a symbiotic relationship. They always seem to know what to do.

My first several months as a mom mirrored that first moment. It was overwhelming, terrifying, stressful, and completely amazing. As the nonbiological mom, I struggled at first to develop a bond with Henry. I attributed this at the time to my lack of biological connection to him as well as my complete ineptitude as a parent. So many people talk about the incredible love they feel towards their children, attributing this feeling to their biological relationship. People say the bond just isn't the same if the baby isn't yours biologically. It's hard not to internalize the angst that those folks may be right. But they're not. The love I feel for Henry is stronger than anything I have ever felt before. It is simply not possible that a stronger bond exists in the universe. He is my world. My heart aches for him when I'm not with him. When I look at his face, I think it is the most beautiful creation on earth, and I want to smoosh him and kiss his cheeks constantly. His smile literally warms my heart. Yet even though I am sure that there is no way I could possibly love him anymore, I still sometimes worry that he won't love me as much because I am not his biological parent.

My wife breastfed Henry, so in addition to being his biological mother, she was also his sole source of nourishment and comfort. In the early months, it often felt like he would never like me and that, maybe, I was even in the way. People told me it would change as he grew older, and it did, but that was very hard to believe at the time. The sleepless nights and endless days made it feel as if there would never be a time that things weren't exactly as they were in that moment. Henry still has times where he just wants his Mama (and nothing can compete with her magic boobies, even well into his toddler years), but he also has moments when he just wants me. We like to play together, read books together, do chores together, run errands together, and he sometimes even wants to cuddle with me. Those fears about not being able to bond and his never loving me enough did turn out to be unfounded, but they still creep into my insecure neurosis periodically. I know the day will come when teenage Henry angrily exclaims, "You're not even my real mother." I'm giving myself more than a decade to prepare a mature intellectual reaction, but I'm pretty sure I will melt into sadness.

Although Henry has noticed when his friends call me the wrong name, he hasn't yet noticed when people think I'm his dad, or what that means, but he will. At two, he has already forced me to rethink the way I interact with people as I walk through the world. For as long as I can remember, I have been mistaken for a boy or a man. When I go into a store, I'm surprised when someone calls me "ma'am" instead of "sir." I never correct them. It has never seemed worth it. It causes confusion, embarrassment, and shame (for everyone involved). It brings up too many memories of bullying and harassment from my childhood. I'd rather stay silent and move on. After all, I don't have any relationship with these people, so why should I bother expending so much emotional energy?

But now I have a son, and this approach no longer feels like the right one. I don't want my boy to grow up feeling as though I hide who I am, and, therefore, he should hide who he is or who his parents are. I no longer navigate the world just for myself. It's now on me to show my child how to navigate the world as well. That is an incredible responsibility.

These incidents are not isolated occurrences. We live in an apartment building in New York City and interact with strangers and neighbours every day. Sometimes, being mistaken for a man gives me a window into male privilege. There is an old man who lives upstairs and only looks and speaks to me—never to my wife. I overheard him once telling another neighbor that my wife and I are both lawyers, but my wife must stay home and watch the baby, even though he sees me take Henry to daycare. There was also the time our neighbour told my wife that her husband (me) helped her carry her dog up the stairs when the elevator was broken. When my wife corrected her and referred to me as her wife, our neighbour stared blankly, seemingly unable to comprehend this reality. (I also didn't actually carry the dog. She carried the dog while I carried her packages.) There is also the woman who works at the bagel store that I have gone to nearly every weekend for five years, who calls me "sir" and the new employee at Henry's daycare who told him to listen to daddy (me). There was the time I wished a woman who works at the supermarket around the corner a Happy Mother's Day, and she responded, "Tell your wife I said Happy Mother's Day." Henry is too young to fully understand these interactions now, but he soon won't be.

Sometimes, people forget and say we look alike or comment on some trait and say that Henry must have gotten that from me. In that simple moment, the epitome of normalcy, the reality of who we are is erased. Once, someone looked at a photo of Henry in my father's office and told my dad that Henry had his eyes. I suppose I should feel happy about those moments because they make it clear that I am Henry's mom. But the biological impossibility of the comments makes them unsettling for me. It feels as though in order to have our connection recognized, we have to fit into the box of biological connectedness.

Then, of course, there are the doctor's appointments and interactions with other professionals, with the inevitable question "Who is the mom?," which always makes me feel as if I'm shrinking into a miniature version of myself like some disappearing queer cartoon character. "We both are," we always reply. But I'm not actually biologically related to Henry, which makes my wife far more valuable when responding to questions about medical history. This fact has the effect of making me feel irrelevant, or at least second class, at doctor's appointments. His genetic history isn't mine. He shares that with my wife and our anonymous sperm donor.

Sometimes, people don't ask. They just look at my wife as though she is obviously the mother of our boy. They assume I am a friend. They look alike, my wife and son. I love that fact. I love that they have the same face. But not looking like either of them sometimes means people assume we're not together, not a family. It also means I look out of place in every family photo, like some giant pale ghost haunting a beautiful and happy mother and child. That certainly comes with the territory of being the nonbiological mom in an interracial lesbian couple, but knowing that doesn't mean it doesn't sting. That the general public looks at us and has a hard time immediately processing our relationship means that we either have to explain it or ignore their ignorance. I am again placed in a position where I feel like I need to expend emotional energy on strangers. My wife, in contrasts, finds it easy and empowering to correct people. Her feeling is that she refuses to have her family erased. I always admire her quick thinking and courage. I am far too introverted and cowardly to follow suit.

Even people who know I'm female don't quite know how to relate to the fact that Henry has two moms. The easiest thing for them to do is put us in the box of a stereotypical heterosexual couple. In that scenario, my wife must be the primary parent and the one in charge of all household chores. I'm the dad who is focused on work, occasionally plays with his kids, and is mainly clueless. So even when people get that we're lesbians, I'm still often saddled with the stereotypes that heteronormativity and toxic masculinity place on dads. These stereotypes negatively affect parents and children by placing everyone in boxes that are hard to break out of. If I'm supposed to be clueless about caring for my kid, why shouldn't I just be clueless and leave the hard stuff of childrearing and homemaking to my wife?

Then there is the inevitable question of "do you want to have a baby?"

This question, of course, means do I want to be pregnant, since I already have a baby. (Well, I did; now I have a big boy who prides himself on the fact that he is getting bigger and bigger and will one day be taller than the trees.) The answer is no, which often seems to trouble people. After all, I have all of the right parts. I have no evidence that I couldn't carry a child to term, but my body doesn't seem built for it. I have a strong suspicion that my body would break—just completely cease to function— if I were to try to use it to make a baby. I've never had a desire to be pregnant. I think it is an amazing, miraculous, brave, and Herculean thing to be able to do. There is nothing more incredible than being able to grow life inside you. It's just not for me.

That feeling also, of course, leads to guilt. As I watched my wife go through the work of trying to get pregnant and then of being pregnant, I felt guilty for not taking the pain from her, for not even being willing to try—all of the waking up at 5:30 a.m. for doctor appointments, hormones, shots, tests, transvaginal ultrasounds, poking and prodding, just to get pregnant, and then the discomfort, pain, and anxiety of being pregnant. It's an incredible thing to be able to do and a marvelous thing to witness. I wished I could share the burden with her. I felt, as all partners of pregnant women must, completely useless and unable to truly help. Consequently, I felt like I couldn't make decisions that involve the process of baby making and pregnancy. How was it my place to have any say? But then was I abdicating my responsibility and leaving her to carry even more weight entirely on her own? This struggle to find my place during pregnancy didn't go away after Henry was born. Figuring out roles that work for all of us requires constant work. Coparenting requires a strong partnership, solid communication, and a regular willingness to do things outside of your comfort zone. In many ways, it's nice not to be completely boxed in by gender stereotypes, even if other people find it easier to put them on us.

Many people assume I have no parenting responsibilities. These are the folks who believe I'm a 1950s man who just comes home to pat his children on the head and occasionally throw a ball around on weekends. Oftentimes, when my wife is out at an event by herself she will get asked who is watching Henry. Her response is always "his other parent." "Oh!" people say in response. I actually think this says more about harmful negative stereotypes that dad's face than it does about queer moms. It's assumed that the father—and, therefore, also the more masculine mother—has an unequal and significantly lesser role in parenting. This is harmful to parents and kids. People rise to the level of our expectations for them. If we set those expectations at zero, we shouldn't be surprised if we don't get much more. If one is expected to be the clueless workaholic, it is easy to fall into that role. That, of course, places a heavy burden on the more feminine partner or biological mother to take on all of the parenting, nurturing, caregiving, and homemaking roles.

This dynamic is also present in interactions with other moms at daycare and on the playground. If my son is doing something I don't want him to do (like refusing to leave daycare because he thinks my arrival is a sign that I am there to play with him and his friends), other moms will often offer friendly advice. Though generally not bad advice, it is always grounded in a sense that I must not know how to manage my toddler and that I need their help. The best is when they tell me something they saw my wife do once. So not only am I not as good at handling my child as they would be, but I'm also not as good as his other mother. I know that all parents receive annoying, unsolicited parenting advice. It does seem more frequent for masculine presenting parents, however.

Implying that all interactions as a nonbiological, masculine-of-centre mom are delegitimizing would be disingenuous. Being a parent also suddenly opens up a whole new world of human interaction. People begin to treat you differently. Neighbours suddenly saw me as a person and became friendly. Just about everyone in our apartment building knows Henry's name (though not mine or my wife's). My coworkers started treating me as a whole human being instead of an unapproachable stone-cold dyke. It's like having a child enters you into this new club of warmth and affection (alongside the judgment and disdain). I imagine the warm interactions only last through the toddler phase, though. Once kids age out of exceptional cuteness, they tend to be viewed as annoyances, instead of joys. It will be interesting to see how these interactions change.

It would also be disingenuous to imply that building new relationships as a mom can't be fabulous. Meeting the parents of Henry's daycare friends has been great. I would not have met them in any other context, and they are lovely, loving people. My family has also expanded because of Henry. We used an anonymous sperm donor to make Henry and have a whole donor sibling family as a result. Henry has several donor siblings. We are in regular communication with two donor brothers, one donor sister, and there are more diblings on the way. It has been wonderful getting to know them and to be able to share some of the joys and challenges of parenting with them. Our donor family is a mix of cultures, sexual orientations, gender identities, and everything else. I feel fortunate that Henry will get to grow up being exposed to different families and family structures.

At first, it was terrifying to meet our dibling families. I was unsure of how to interact with them or what the expectations would be. We connected with them through the donor sibling registry (DSR). My wife joined the DSR during her first pregnancy, which ended in miscarriage. At the time, we learned of one family who lived in a different state. We had a brief but pleasant exchange through the DSR messaging feature. After the miscarriage, my wife did not return to the DSR for a long time. Then one day, while she was getting a haircut, she decided to log back in. It turns out there was a message from another family, so she reached out to them. A day or so later, she received a message saying that two families were going to be meeting the following weekend, and we were invited. At that point, Henry was eleven months old.

I'll never forget when my wife got that message. We were visiting my parents, and I remember standing in their kitchen as she read the message aloud. OMG! We had to say yes. We only had a few days to process what these new relationships might be like and what we would tell Henry. We obsessively googled everything we could about them, which led us to convince ourselves for a couple of days that one of the moms was a semifamous right-wing demagogue and completely panicked. It turns out they just share a common name. I remember walking in to the host family's apartment and seeing people snapping photos as the kids met each other for the first time. I think I went mute. But everyone was so kind and loving, and we all slowly opened up to each other. They even had a birthday cake for Henry.

A few months later, we heard from another family who also used the same sperm donor. We immediately began texting each other. "Will it scare them if we tell them we're one big giant happy family already?" "Ok, let's take it slow, so we don't spook them." Now we all communicate via text message regularly and get together periodically. We text about funny things our kids do and say. We text about medical issues and particular ailments our kids have experienced. We also text about legal issues, including second-parent adoption.

As a lawyer, of course, I'm trained to spot legal issues, and the diminution of legal issues is also certainly something to feel happy about. Since before Henry was born, we talked about doing a second-parent adoption so that I would be sure to have a legal relationship to my son in case anything terrible were to happen. We researched case law and found, as the *New York Times* described, that not long before Henry was born, a lesbian mom in Brooklyn was denied a second-parent adoption because she was legally married to her wife and, thus, the child was a child of the marriage. The court said that since New York had a presumption that a child of the marriage is a child of both members of the married couple, and since same-sex marriage was now recognized nationally, there was no need for the second-parent adoption (McKinley). Although the judge's reasoning was progressive and should have given us hope, it made us nervous. We felt as though we could not file a second-parent adoption petition because it would be thrown out, yet we didn't quite feel confident enough that the judge was correct that it would never be an issue when there was a child of a marriage. The election of Donald Trump made us even more nervous, and pushed us to actually get the second-parent adoption.

Yet thinking about the legal dangers, and legal possibilities, I can't help but feel grateful to be a nonbiological mother at this time. If I had been a bit older and met my wife a little bit earlier, my wife and I would not have been able to get legally married. As it stands, when we first met and began dating, neither of us was sure we would ever be able to get married. We rejoiced together when New York State recognized gay marriage and then when the U.S. Supreme Court extended that recognition nationally. (In fact, I remember distinctly the moment when sitting with my then-girlfriend watching the New York State legislature debate gay marriage I realized I should have been saving up money for an engagement ring.) We navigated purchasing sperm from an anonymous donor and using it for artificial insemination with relative ease. No one questioned our relationship throughout that process, although we would have run into some hurdles had we decided to use a known donor. Yet before we filed for formal adoption papers, I didn't worry regularly that someone is going to question my relationship with Henry and try to take him away from me. I don't have to fear that the state is going to declare me an unfit parent because I am a lesbian. For that, and for this moment of social progress, (even if it feels like our enemies are winning on every other front), I am even more grateful to be Henry's mom right now.

Navigating the world is messy. Henry is a biracial, Jewish, son of lesbians. Merely existing as himself is going to mean, at best, facing questions from curious onlookers and, at worst, vitriol and hate. It's up to his mothers to teach him how to be an intelligent, kind, and confident person in a world filled with racism, sexism, and heteronormativity. But how can I do that if I haven't quite figured out how to walk through the world that way myself? I don't quite have the answer, but I do know that being Henry's mom is the best thing that ever happened to me, so I keep trying to figure it out.

I thought that by the time I wrote this chapter, I would have more figured out—some wonderful story to tell about how Henry made me live more authentically 100 per cent of the time. The truth is that it's still a struggle. It turns out I parent with all of the anxieties and insecurities I have always possessed. Instead of ridding myself of insecurities, I have gained whole new ones related to whether I am a good enough mom to Henry and whether I am doing enough to show the world what different families can look like. My hope is that my awareness of these traits means that I won't pass them along to Henry, so that he can always be his most authentic self, no matter what obstacles he faces. Maybe accepting myself as a mom is good enough for now. My hope is that some of my story has resonated with you and that all of it reassures you that whatever your experience is as a parent, it is beautiful, unique, and groundbreaking. If we continue to live out loud and raise our kids to be better people than we are, the world will keep moving forwards.

Endnotes

1. This is my favorite verse from Brandi Carlile's "The Mother":

   You are not an accident where no one thought it through
   The world has stood against us, made us mean to fight for you
   And when we chose your name we knew that you'd fight the
   power too. You're nothing short of magical and beautiful to me
   Oh, I'll never hit the big time without you
   So they can keep their treasure and their ties to the machine
   'Cause I am the mother of Evangeline

Works Cited

Carlile, Brandi. "Brandi Carlile—The Mother (Live)." *YouTube*, 14 Dec. 2017, www.youtube.com/watch?v=z865nKpgH0Q. Accessed 9 July 2020.

McKinley, James C. Jr. "Judge Alarms Gay Parents in Denying Legal Adoption." *New York Times,* 28 Jan. 2014, p. A17.

Chapter Fifteen

Queering Biology through the "Glue of Love"

Sonja Mackenzie

When my daughter was four, she came home from preschool recounting an interaction she had with her friend that day. He proclaimed that all families have a mum and a dad. She stated that this was not so: "I have a mama and a mommy. I have a donor, not a daddy." My daughter has always been open about her family, as we are with her. The two children pondered this, and then continued on with their elaborate game of animal families. Best friends in their exploration of the world, the two children were unwittingly engaged in a conversation that strikes at the core of current debates about kinship and queer families.

At the centre of these debates lie heteronormative tropes premised on notions of biology, which are resisted yet also often reinforced in queer family formations. As a queer parent straddling both biological and nonbiological relationships with my two children, I find that biology lies as an uneasy marker and prefer instead to invoke alternative understandings of what my daughter has named the "glue of love" as central to queer family formations. This does not naively deny the physiological realities of biology, nor does it accord biology the cultural authority that we queer families so often grant it. This chapter explores some of the questions, tensions and opportunities that biology raises for queer communities.

I first became a parent twelve years ago, when the queer parent nomenclature was marked by its "non" status. Indeed, "nonbiological" and "nongestational" were the best, if not the only, names for the specific parenting role I was embarking on at the time. This initial entry into parenting was marked with joy, all the usual forms of anxiety and anticipation, and many of the not-so-usual forms of feeling societally invisible, misunderstood, and vulnerable as a nonbiological queer parent. Three years later, I gave birth to our second child, becoming a second-time parent through a first-time bodily experience of carrying a pregnancy and giving birth. Along the way, I have identified primarily as a nonbiological parent, as it was in that profoundly formative role that I initially moved into parenthood. So many of my interactions with the world outside as a parent are marked by perceptions of family that are expressions of society's simultaneous fascination with and tensions about biology and queerness. Biologizing narratives become a safe way to stabilize what others can't quite comprehend. LGBTQ families are, by definition, queering biology through subverting heteronormative family structures.

But what does this mean as a queer parent? In what ways can queering family be something that we take on with more reflectiveness as part of our collective family projects? I hope in the pages that follow to be able to provide insight through personal experience as well as my work on gender and sexuality on what it might look like to queer biology. There are myriad forms of nonbiological kinship in the queer community. My family reflects just one through our configuration of two unmarried white mums—one American born and raised with a nine-year period living in Spain and one born and raised in rural Scotland, who recently became an American citizen—one identity-release donor; and two (amazing!) mixed-race white and Latinx children of Scottish, Spanish, Mexican, Ecuadorian, Danish, Italian, and German heritage. Our journey to our family structure is another story for another time, but suffice it to say, we explored for a couple of years various options concerning donor type on our journey to parenthood (including known, partially known or friend of a friend, and sperm bank). Once we settled on a sperm bank, we sorted through various factors for selecting our donor, including their familial background, their philosophical, social and emotional values, as well as physiological factors that resonated with our own ancestry.

This chapter describes a personal set of experiences; it does not aim to represent or reflect all possible family configurations. I am also keenly aware of the many forms of pregnancy and infant or child loss that can accompany journeys to parenthood, and write this chapter aware of what a privilege being a parent can be. Finally, I write with deep respect for queer families that do not involve children and believe that queering biology also involves decoupling children from family. Being a family does not require having children, as so many of our queer families illustrate through their diverse kinship configurations and intimacies. Indeed, being a parent has underscored the ways in which parenting is not some essential human state or way to realize self-hood; it is but one avenue through which to experience states of human connection as well as that familial construct of love, which queer families realize in so many ways. Although this chapter involves some of my reflections on parenting, I do not equate family with being a parent or having children. Families are intimate spaces that are inherently created through our own philosophies as well as our shared values and understandings. They also reflect broader social tensions and meanings about inclusion and belonging while comprising one of the most basic economic units fuelling our postindustrial, capitalist society. LGBTQ families are not outside of these social contexts, yet we have created unique family formations that call into question much of their basic premises, often through spoken and unspoken biological narratives.

What does it mean to navigate two forms of biological relationships in a family? Although such a question is hardly a new one—as families, queer and otherwise, are constructed through varied and complex forms of kinship—standing at this nexus brings to light possibilities for queering family and biology simultaneously. Ultimately, I am the same parent to each of my children—the one who holds down the routine of our children's lives, the boring "have-you-had-your shower?" mama, and the holder of the details of what form is due when. I am the same snuggle-at-night (but not endlessly) mama, the one not blessed with the never-ending patience of my partner, the proud one who gets teary-eyed at the sound of my children's music. Yet parts of the parenting experience have been unique—most significantly, as a nonbiological parent, having to work that much harder in those initial months and years as a soon-to be and new parent to be recognized just as a parent, even by well-meaning family and community members.

Carrying our second child was a new experience through the physiological realities of pregnancy, but, and perhaps more profoundly, it spoke to the deep meanings that continue to underlie my experience as a nonbiological parent. I am grateful that I was able to experience the strange and painful beauty of pregnancy and, particularly, birth, yet the cultural credence afforded to me and my large belly was both deeply affirming and profoundly troubling. I grieved not only the loss of our family of three but also what I had known for some time: I was now perceived by too many as a real parent for the first time. This situation raised a shocking new set of insights for me, and it's in this space of reflection at the interface of being both biological and nonbiological parent that I share insights about being a nonbiological parent and the queer possibilities of parenting.

Biology is undeniable, yet how does it assume meaning for queer families? How do parents and children navigate understandings of what it means to be family in a world premised on essential notions of biological determinism without naively denying the embodied realities that DNA present? How does the interface of reproductive technologies and queer communities, including that of donor siblings, reinforce hegemonic biological constructs of family? And how do we unintentionally reify the very constructs we have the ability to challenge through practices of daily familial life? This essay will explore these questions through an in-depth reflection on the threads of similarities and differences of being simultaneously nonbiological and biological. I suggest that biology is a queer space—a space where clear binary renderings may prove incomplete and where there are powerful ways to shift not just understandings but practices of being in families based on what matters most.

Becoming a Parent and the Role of the State

Engaging biology as a queer space for LGBTQ families necessitates locating the family unit in the systems of social stratification that it reflects and reproduces. Families have always been political and contested terrain as well as a space for state involvement. In the United States (U.S.), racist strategies of forcing the separation of parents and children have their roots in the colonial racial project of the country to build and maintain white supremacy. This project has been evident since the earliest days of colonialism; Black children were separated from their parents through chattel slavery, as they were sold and traded as commodities, and Indigenous children were separated from their families and made to attend boarding schools in the late nineteenth and early twentieth century. These painful histories are currently being revisited—not that they ever went away—as the U.S. separates primarily Latino undocumented immigrant children from their families, detains them in cages, and systematically abuses them. Who gets to be a family is not neutral terrain, as some family forms are privileged over others—something communities of colour know all too well through the ongoing surveillance and interference of the state into family affairs as well as through foster care and adoption systems that reinforce white privilege.

Despite the historic same-sex marriage ruling in the U.S. in 2015, parental rights are not necessarily a given in queer married families, so queer parents in the U.S. must still go through the humiliating and problematic process of adopting the children we have planned for, helped to conceive, and raised. Furthermore, homophobic agendas currently threaten queer families in the U.S. through legislation that, if approved, would make it legal to ban queer parents from adopting. This so-called religious freedom, anti-LGBT adoption amendment would affect any parents whom a taxpayer-funded adoption agency objects to—same-sex parents, divorced parents, single parents, inter-faith parents—and represents a devastating setback for queer families and those of us outside of the white, two-parented, Christian, and heterosexual family norm. As those of us who have known what it is to navigate this tenuous space of questioned parenting, these are concrete and ever-present realities.

One of the most challenging experiences for me as a nonbiological parent in my early days of coming into parenting was having to adopt my daughter. We went through second-parent adoption procedures in my daughter's first year, and despite living in an LGBTQ hub and working with a progressive adoption agency known for its work with LGTQ families, the systematic, institutional undermining of my role as a parent was heartbreaking. Although many queer parents celebrate adoption day with pictures of babies and family in the arms of friendly magistrates, I wondered what indeed there was to celebrate, since I had been made to adopt my child. At that point in our child's short life, my partner had returned to work, and I was essentially the primary parent. I cared for my daughter during the day while conducting research for my dissertation and teaching as well as I could with a baby who was a mediocre sleeper at best. Despite the challenges of these days, my daughter and I came to pattern our lives closely with one another; I would pass her off to a friendly grandparent while pursuing my work, scooping her up after a few hours. I could predict her every want, and I was the one she turned to when she had a need. I have always understood parenting preferences, to the extent that they have come up in our family, as driven by time spent with the child rather than biology.

So when I had to turn to friends to request three letters of support to attest to my ability to parent my daughter and when I had to reveal my religious affiliation and every last detail of my economic viability, it sickened me to consider that the symbiotic relationship I was in with my child was being questioned. That my friends had to offer up stories of observing my parenting competencies and that a social worker had to come and observe me with my daughter one fall morning, despite her assurances that it was just pro forma, caused me nothing short of distress and many sleepless nights. And ours was an easier process, since we knew that the adoption agency was essentially on our side and the judge would rule that I was, at the end of every meticulous form completed and every home observation rendered, fit to be a parent. But still, what if my daughter rejected me that morning under the observant eye of the trained social worker? What if this state-run process would reveal that in fact I was not a "real" parent? It was devastating to know that I had to prove myself to the state by virtue of my nonbirth status; I began to question my own worthiness as a parent along the lines of biology.

It is impossible to erase the deep marks of the initial role of the state in defining (that is, questioning) my parenthood by virtue of my nonbiological relationship to my child. The ongoing need for adoption proceedings for queer parents to adopt our children, despite popular misunderstandings that queer marriage is, in fact, the same as heterosexual marriage, continues to create a nonbiological second-class parent status. As a non-US citizen at the time, I was also aware of the privilege afforded me by the whiteness of my skin. Yet raising multi-racial children as a queer family at a time when families around us are being torn apart by the state is a constant reminder of the various and intersecting axes of oppression upon which families are surveilled and punished in the U.S. daily. Queering biology represents an ongoing effort to decouple parenthood from the social, legal, and economic meanings that play themselves out through biology.

Becoming a Parent: Part One

Biology is a queer thing. We configure our families with incredible diversity by intention and necessity. We are forced to consider how we may want to be, how we can be, what we can afford, what our understandings of biology and genetics are, and what comprises a family from the earliest days of envisioning our families. Our trajectories to parenting are rarely linear and often involve grappling with multiple feelings of marginalization from the very heteronormative family structures that often oppressed and shunned us. This is confusing. Why can't we just mindlessly procreate, as so many of our heterosexual brothers and sisters can do, which allows them to evade difficult dialogues, personal reflections, and, if in a relationship, the intimate and familial relationship dynamics that having children engender. We spend endless amounts of emotional energy and financial resources to reach a point at which we know, with as much certainty as one ever can, that we will be welcoming a child into our families. This wears on us. I remember feeling deeply angry that we had to grapple with the ethical questions of donor selection—a privileged position to have as we had to have the finances to enter this industry—and hearing the counsel that we, as queers, get to start the life-changing experience of parenting that will continue for decades to come, even before we know anything about who we are doing this for. Parents make profoundly ethical life decisions daily for—and later with—our children, and queers just get a head start on this. Great, I remember thinking. It was not exactly reassuring, and, if anyone cares, I'm still angry. So, biology rears its head from our earliest hopes, desires and visions of how to create our families.

"Beautiful baby! Her ears look just like yours!" This comment – likely generous in intent - was more a statement about meanings of parenthood than anything else. I was holding my month-old daughter in my arms in a far-too-long line at our favourite bakery in San Francisco after a follow up visit to the midwife. Chocolate croissants and warm tea were the rewards for making the long drive with our newborn across the Bay on that blustery winter morning, and we were excited to introduce her to a mainstay of our old neighbourhood. We were in the throes of those early, bleary and semi out-of-this-world days of newborn life with an only child, where the days and nights stretch together in one long series of basic human bodily functions alongside never-ending and amazing physical connection. My partner and I were still both off work and able to revel in those pleasures of slowly becoming a family of three – the long wait in line for ridiculously expensive chocolate pastries or the stroll around town with no destination or goal but rather just to watch our baby settle her eyes on something for the first time, whether a horizon, a leaf, or a new color. Total perfection.

I had noticed that the person behind me in line at the café had spent the better part of the past fifteen minutes looking at my daughter, as many did in those days, lulled into the captivating world of the placid newborn, the wisdom of that new but wise old-person face, still close to other places it seemed. But something was different with the gaze of this stranger. She was taking in more than the sleepy baby, more than the predictable read of gender. She was sizing up our place in the world, finding words to define this child and the parent in whose arms it slept. It wasn't the first time I had experienced this in my short month as a parent, and I had also felt it in the months leading up to parenthood: It was that feeling of being sized up, of being stated and created in a way that made sense to the viewer. Yet when she made the comment, the absurdity of the likeness of an ear was clear to us both. I looked at her, smiled in that postpartum blissed out state, and just said, "Yes, isn't she perfect."

Yet the comment sat with me. It was based on a compulsion to find likeness, to locate parenthood in a physiological expression. The comment assumed that I must have birthed this child to have earned my place there in line, holding her. It was benign and yet, at its core, painful. I couldn't shrug it off as merely one ignorant person. I found that it cut to the core of who I was, how I perceived myself in these tender days of coming into a relationship with my child and into an understanding of myself as a parent. The overlay of biology was clear here. In those early days of parenthood, I was also aware of the child in my literal and figurative arms. Before my child could understand these words explicitly, I could get away with not correcting this person, not explicitly stating who I was and my relationship to my child. Although I do not believe that I owe anyone any explanation, I have always been compelled to speak the truth of my experiences around my children, and now that they are older, each instance of a misunderstanding (or, rather, a misproclamation) is an opportunity to make sure that we get to be seen as nonbiological parents or queer families. To this day, the statement that "Her dad must be so tall" is something I hear often when my (tall) partner is not around, to which I usually respond, "Yes, she gets her height from her other mom." It is important that my daughter hears that our family is not just there to be understood through heteronormative eyes but to be seen for and as who we are. These reactions do not result in major political changes, nor do they ultimately matter to anyone other than me, but, perhaps, my children are learning about the importance of decoupling family from biology as well as the importance of being visible as a queer family even in the banality of the everyday. As a parent, all I can hope for is that my children are taking it in, paying attention, and will be part of a future generation of change makers and justice seekers, which our world increasingly needs.

Becoming a Parent: Part Two

I have always wanted to be a parent. Growing up, I worked with children and families affected by HIV/AIDS in the mid-1990s at a time when antiretroviral medications were just starting to lengthen lives. Despite medical advances, we were still surrounded by death. Many of us, as young queers, worked closely with families who had children with HIV, either by birth or adoption; we tried to forge informal support systems where there was limited institutional support. We reveled in the joys of another day, perhaps another year, and I was driven to surround myself with children. Although I did not go on to open a home for children living with HIV, which was my dream during college, I always knew I wanted children of my own. When I met my partner, we shared this as a vision for our future, and since she was older and knew that she wanted to carry a pregnancy, we decided that she would carry our child. As our daughter grew, my partner was the one to press for a sibling; I felt that life was complete with one child and couldn't imagine anything being better. Why change something if it's working? Could we afford it? We could barely pay for preschool as it was. Why bring another child into a world heavy with burden and grief? But the pull was strong for my partner, so I reconsidered, and once we decided that we would pursue having a second child, I was both excited and also cautious to move into the experience of carrying this child. How would this change my relationship with my daughter? What if I hated pregnancy? A few months after I completed my doctoral degree, I became pregnant with our second child.

I both loved and hated pregnancy. We joked that pregnancy with a first child is like a luxury vacation compared to pregnancy with a second child. When my partner was pregnant, I would tend to her, massaging her feet and helping to assuage the nausea she felt so terribly. This was not to be during my pregnancy, and keeping up with our active two-year-old was a constant challenge alongside my ever-growing belly and utter exhaustion. In many ways, I felt that I missed out on fully getting to be pregnant, a state that I enjoyed in itself, but one I wished that I could have experienced with more ease. I had all the first-time experiences of physical pregnancy but with the added bonus of my first child developing a sense of will and independence that consumed every ounce of my emotional presence. Carrying this second child allowed me to experience firsthand what I had taken in but not directly experienced the first time, such as the fact that people can and do feel that they can engage with a pregnant body and make comments—"Oh, it's a boy! A big boy!"—or offer a seat to a pregnant person on an overcrowded subway. It served as a painful validation—from the other side—of the ways I had systematically been excluded from expecting my child as an invisible parent-to-be with my daughter. And then, of course, there were the not insignificant number of people who expressed their delight that I was now going to have a child, a clear indication that they did not perceive me to be a full parent to my first child. Saddened, I went home to my amazing and demanding toddler who sucked every last ounce of my energy daily; a constant reminder that I was, indeed, a full parent.

Pregnancy represented a transition from nonbiological parenthood to something new—a straddling of both forms of parenthood. I was aware that my biological status also brought with it my partner's nonbiological status, an experience I understood well. The physical and emotional states of pregnancy have been a shared experience within our relationship. My partner was able to anticipate my needs and understand my aches and pains. And when I could barely walk in the weeks up to our second child's birth, she completely understood the feeling in a way that only someone who has been brought to their knees by the physiological experience of carrying another human being can. Biological parents in the queer community have privilege that needs to be broken down and understood within—as well as outside of—queer relationships to maintain equity and to truly challenge normative biological tropes so often internalized and reproduced within the queer community. I am unendingly grateful to my partner for recognizing that with her desire and our decision for her to carry our first child, she was entering into a parenting relationship with me that granted her cultural credibility and social license to be a parent, while I was rendered the "other mother." Her active role in decentring this narrative came through many seemingly minor but significant decisions and actions we took with our first child, many of which carried over into our second child.

Every one of the baby-preparation-focused classes—and it's quite the overwhelming industry, even on the mindfulness and home-birth circuit we were on—equates pregnancy with being a parent and, more specifically, a mother. In each one of these venues, despite my best efforts, I could not find a space that spoke to my specific experience. An informal group of second-time parents became a long-standing form of support, yet in the months leading up to birth, I found myself to be alienated from the body talk and knowledge of my peers, as my body had not experienced birth yet. I yearned to feel camaraderie and meet someone who had a similar experience—someone who understood the experience of having a first-time pregnant body with the joys and burdens of a second time child. Yet I could not bring physical knowing to my days of preparing for birth alongside other second-time parents. So perhaps I belonged more with the tentative and anxious first-time parents as they stepped into their first birth, with birth plans, homemade essential oils, and music playlists that I knew would likely never be used. As intense and physically all-consuming supporting a birth is, it is just not the same as the earth- and body-shattering physical experience of childbirth, so I found myself fearful of giving birth yet possessing more knowledge of what was to come than the other first timers. I was also afraid to lose my relationship with my daughter and knew that the physical demands of nursing would likely shift the closeness of our connection, but I also thought this might also be a good thing in the overall schema of our family. And so it was with soft tears running down my check that I experienced labour surrounded by the semistillness of our home, reading our daughter her last book as an only child between contractions, knowing that our worlds were about to change forever. As much as I was grieving this relationship in advance, I was also unknowingly mourning the loss of the beauty of my time as solely a nonbiological parent.

"Crisscross": Parenting beyond Babyhood

Becoming both a biological and a nonbiological parent has not necessarily been easier than being just a nonbiological parent, and this is not just about how much more overwhelming it is having two children. Giving birth was beyond anything I had ever imagined. It changed my understanding of my body and of the human body. It was inexplicable in its power and peace all at once. Coming back from feeling close to death, of feeling such proximity to otherworldly sensation, was something I could never imagine. And, indeed, nursing our son changed our family relationships considerably, as predicted. Our daughter oriented much more to my partner, who was more available to her, since I was consumed with the demands of nursing. And so we entered the sweet chaos of life as four. I missed having coherent conversations with my partner, as well as a more predictable relationship, even as I marvelled at her in new ways. I missed my daughter and the way things were, and I cherished my son as well; surprisingly, or not, love is expansive and grows as families do.

One thing we did anticipate and have experienced since our second's arrival is the ongoing comments and institutional feedback that once again narrated for us the biological dimensions of our family. Our son is a "mini-me," although I don't quite see it this way. Yet, apparently, this alleged resemblance was worthy of comment each and every time people saw us together throughout his infancy and beyond. He is musical; oh, it must be my family. My daughter is artistic; it must be my partner's heritage. People hear and seek out biological explanations for everything from physical traits to life passions and interests. Although we don't deny the physiological realities of genetics, we have intentionally resisted these biological narratives as part of our parenting. We talk openly with our children about our family origins, and although I would like to think that we have influenced their critical thinking about families, in many ways, this has originated organically from them.

One evening, after yet another instance of explaining our family to a first-grade classmate, my daughter came home and proclaimed that our family was actually "crisscross." "What do you mean by this?" I asked. "Crisscross," she said. "You know, I am like mama but came from mommy's body. I have straight hair and am more, well, kind of shy. Brother—he's got that curly hair and is always bubbly, just like mommy. But he was born from your body." She paused. "Well, what do you think makes a family?" my partner enquired. My daughter sat still, pondering this question, then, with her big, bright six-year-old eyes looked up and stated: "It's the glue of love. It's a love string that connects me to you." She continued to narrate our crisscross family structure through several forms—including the zippy version of zigzag—and still comes back to these as frameworks for understanding biology. These forms not only resist normative understandings of families but also highlight the foundational role biology plays in creating families. Zigzag. Crisscross. All held together by the glue of love. This is our family through and through.

Much of the parenting guidance literature orients to infancy and early childhood—perhaps because these are the only years in which we actually have time to read a chapter or skim the relevant pages to absorb what is needed before the next demand on our time. In many ways, time becomes more elusive as children get older—"big kids, big issues; little kids, little issues," as one wise friend once said to us in the early years as we were complaining about sleep deprivation while her teenager had just crashed the family car. This was certainly the case for me. I vividly recall researching, purchasing, and voraciously reading each of the queer parenting manuals I had bought in any free moment as we prepared for our first child, including how-to books or more personal narratives, especially on nonbiological parenting. Although it was reassuring to know that we were not alone in our various and queer forms of agonizing over our children, many of these stories of queer nonbiological parenting actually reinforced a sense of second-class citizenship through essentialist narratives of biological determinism and othering, which I found upsetting. They further marginalized me as I came to my own queer parent identity.

Maybe the stories of parenting older children are few and far between because we know that, ultimately, there are few things such guidance books can really affect, particularly as our kids become more themselves in the world. Maybe our worlds become more heteronormatively oriented as we become more and more embedded in those foundational institutions of childhood—schools, the PTA, sports teams. We come to be the queer representative on whatever committee needs one and find, time and again, a role voicing our queer parenting experience in the broader world of primarily heterosexually parented families. We don't want to read about families because we are busy being families and anticipating how we or our children may need to explain ourselves. So we are tired. Perhaps as our children orient more to their peers and the world outside, parents can turn our attention away from the finer, somewhat mind-numbing details of parenting. The labour of parenting cannot and should not be our everything, which it felt like in those early days. For whatever reason, the transition into older childhood is far less documented in parenting literatures as well as in queer literatures, as are the experiences of nonbiological parents. Yet perhaps they should be. These are, in many ways, some of the most formative years for children, and these are times of media saturation and increasing social fragmentation—when our queer communities and children need our attention more than ever.

"Alligators were all coming to eat me," our eight-year-old says as he leans into me after crawling into bed after a nightmare. "So many of them," he says. It's the end of the school year; changes are ahead, and it's all happening in his dream world right now. We snuggle, finding comfort from all imaginings of the night, and I wonder why he came to my side of the bed. Is it because I gave birth to him? What about when our daughter goes to my partner in the middle of the night and not to me? Are there biological connections that are so deeply embedded that they are undeniable in these tender and unplanned moments of life? Whatever the answers to these questions, the fact that we carry these questions in our daily (and nightly) parenting lives tells us something about the meanings of biology in a mixed family such as ours. Queer parenting demands far more of us than merely bringing comfort after our children have nightmares. Queer parenting requires that we face the constancy of questions not just from the outside world but from our deepest and innermost selves. These questions include the daily insecurities of parenting, enforced through institutions, family, and peers—enhanced with a healthy dose of what does biology mean each and every day.

I lead the way to his room, as requested, to make sure that all ghosts and night creatures have to wrestle with me first. I shift out of my own thoughts of biology, love, and what makes a family and focus on the sweet tousle-haired child now in the softness of his own bed. I hand him his stuffed mushroom, one of his favourite toys. "Your mushroom," I whisper, Your mushroom with its big cap and love-filled eyes will bat away all the bad dreams, I promise you my love." And sleep arrives.

Queering the Sibling Relationship

Donor siblings—or "diblings" as they have rather inanely come to be called—have become an important part of the biologizing of queer kinship. Donor siblings refer to children who share the same sperm donor but who are raised in different families. Technically, my two children share the same donor but are being raised in the same family, so we refer to them as siblings, not donor siblings. As such, donor siblings have become an important part of kinship and a mechanism through which understandings of family and biology become produced, a means of queering biology for LGBTQ families. Although a full consideration of siblinghood in queer families is beyond the scope of this chapter, I wish to briefly consider how the pull of donor siblings reflects and perpetuates a biological frame for understanding familial relationships while also presenting queer possibilities for families.

More and more, families who use donor sperm are contacting other families who have used the same donor by signing up with a $99 membership fee to be part of a national database known as the donor sibling registry (DSR). Families can then search for their donor by identification number and sperm bank, and then connect with other families who have used the same donor. Fairly simple, it would appear, yet this is only the beginning of a profound family-making experience that centres on specific biological understandings of what makes a sibling.

Why do people do this? The reasons for seeking donor siblings are many. For some, contacting donor sibling families is a way to connect with other children who share a partial genetic makeup; for others, it may provide a way to learn more about certain health traits of their children; and others may seek sibling relationships for children who do not have siblings in their own families or, if they do, to build additional familial relationships based on shared biology. Time and again, queer parents have revealed to me the powerful connections that they experience when seeing their children's donor siblings from physical traits and expressions—from the dark shock of hair on their child to the soft reach of a glance—to shared interests and the overall look of a sibling. Time and again, people attest to the unspoken connections that donor siblings have that transcend time or quality of relationship and, importantly yet quietly, inscribe lines of biological kinship. Time and again, it seems that parents are the ones seeking diblings and the meanings they create.

Yet I am curious as to the meanings that this process holds for children as they begin to understand what makes a family as well as for nonbiological parents in particular, whose lines of connection to their child reveal that family is far more than biology. How do nonbiological parents navigate the centring of the biological relationship that the dibling comes to assume and represent? How do children understand siblings if not as those children who share their home and their parent(s)—that glue of love that forms families? The memories of that time when the family rolled down the snowy hill together; the smell of home, the attic; the time when big sister rescued brother from that overgrown oak tree that looked doable on the way up; the knowing glance between siblings as they tolerate, barely, their tired parent's grumpy evening rant. The knowing. The sweetness and the angst. This is the stuff of siblinghood.

Diblings may sound cute, but I wonder what the pursuit of the dibling relationship is doing to our ability to understand siblinghood, and indeed family, as a set of experiences and connections rather than as a biological fact. Although donor siblings present an expansive set of familial relationships, and of course open up their own set of experiences and connections, they are premised on biological connection, not the minutia of daily life, which, ultimately, family life is all about. Our children know about the DSR, and if and when they wish to identify donor siblings, we will gladly support them in pursuing these connections. Until then, we ask them to tell us what makes a sibling to them, and they say, well, they're pretty happy with the sibling they already have.

Centring Queer Voices

This generation of queer families in the U.S. has been traversing the journey to and though parenthood though some of the most significant legal and cultural shifts our society has witnessed in recent history. Although our legitimacy remains fragile in many pockets of the country, marriage remains—even, and perhaps especially, for queers—an economic and legal institution upon which society is structured and social legitimacy is granted (not to mention the concrete markers of physical health and emotional wellbeing that are tied to legal marital status). The fact that the illegitimate status of queer-parented children (i.e., their status as being born out of wedlock) was used as a key part of the legal argument in the gay marriage Supreme Court case while persistent racism deems Black and Brown children born out of wedlock still as illegitimate reveals the extent to which some children—including, now, LGBTQ-parented children—are deemed worthy of marriage's legal and social legitimacy. Yet as queer parents we need the over one-thousand legal and economic benefits of marriage to protect our children, so we face a situation in which many of us move into marriage to secure these protections and benefits. In our everyday lives, however, we know that our family still lives with the many and varied forms of heterosexism and homophobia that continue to play out in schools, playgrounds, homes, and around the dinner table. The conversation at these tables, around kids' activities and in daily parenting life, has shifted.

Yet in my experience, in this increased acceptance and (semi) coolness of queerness, there is still a tendency to talk over and through queer experiences. We are now a "thing," a commodity that circulates around cafeteria tables and about which everyone has a story. Furthermore, the unknowns of biological origins raise questions and anxieties that are more about broader social anxieties of kinship rather than being about our families. People are fascinated by queer families, yet they don't quite know how to engage us. As such, here are a few tips that may resonate with other nonbiological families in particular; they are also for the many and wonderful well-meaning people who have questions about my crisscross family.

First, my partner is not my wife. Just because I can marry her does not mean that I will. I am concerned about this profoundly sexist and racist institution, which means I will not participate in it. This is a privileged position from which to speak and often results in critical comments from queers around us. Please don't assume that all of us in the LGBTQ community are promarriage or willing to be wives by referring to my life partner as my wife. Second, please do ask questions—we welcome questions in our family—but don't ask me questions about my kids in front of them. Please ask them questions if you want to learn about them. We have followed the advice given by Our Family Coalition and other queer family organizations to "tell early, tell often" so that our kids have the language to understand their own experiences and to respond when the inevitable questions come up. So, they are remarkably at ease in addressing your list of questions or your discomfort. Just ask.

Third, if you do ask me how my kids came to be, expect that you should render a similar story about your own kids' origins. All children have biological origins and stories. Just as the all-too-often unspoken dominant paradigms of whiteness and masculinities are the norm around which understandings of race and gender circulate, heterosexual biologies are the (unspoken) norm. Yet they are still there. There are biological choices and considerations that configure all journeys to parenthood, and we need to decentre the powerful axes of privilege held within heterosexist assumptions about parenthood and the ways in which biology serves as a powerful motor of this privilege. Fourth, please don't speak over me as I talk with you about these intimate life moments. I don't need to be commodified as you excitedly tell me how you have met another donor child when we are talking about my children, nor do I need to hear how you heard of someone who chose to be a surrogate for a heterosexual family to help a family in need. Stay on topic. Most of all, and finally, listen. Let queer—and specifically nonbiological queer—voices be the ones at the fore of our families. We are here but often invisible. We have many and varied stories to tell if you are able to hear them. Let us consider with you the queering of biology that our family formations can render.

As this volume suggests, queer nonbiological parents have unique experiences that are also very much the same as the usual medley of humdrum and joy shared by all parents, no matter the journey to and through parenthood. Even as we must consider the voices of queer parents reflecting on biology, I have tried to consider here the implications of biology—and specifically queering biology—for broadening our understandings and experiences of kinship and parenthood in queer families and beyond. In so doing, I have hoped to provide a vision of how queer families can continue to truly subvert dominant paradigms of biology and bring forward a vision—both within our own families and for the benefit of all families—for the glue of love my daughter spoke so tenderly of years ago, emphasizing connection and kinship in a world struggling to understand what matters most.

Notes on Contributors

Melissa Boyce resides in central California with her wife Erin. She works in sales—a career that has allowed her to exercise her desire to meet and talk to new people. Melissa enjoys spending time with family and friends, going to the movies, playing and watching sports, as well as attending any rock concert she can. She and Erin attend local LGBTQ events and are a part of an LGBTQ parents' group where they spend time with other same-sex families. Among all of Melissa's favorite things, the best part of her life is spending time with her wife and raising their four-year-old daughter together.

Jax Jacki Brown is a disability and LGBTIQ rights activist, writer and educator based in Melbourne, Australia. Jax holds a BA in Cultural Studies and Communication where they examined the intersections between disability and LGBTIQ identities and their respective rights movements. Jax has written for *Junkee, Daily Life, The Feminist Observer, Writers Victoria, ABC's Ramp Up, Hot Chicks with Big Brains, and Archer Magazine: The Australian Journal for Sexual Diversity.* Jax is published in the following anthologies: *Queer Disability Anthology* (2015), *Doing It: Women Tell the Truth about Great Sex* (2016), *QueerStories: Reflections on Lives Well Lived from Some of Australia's Finest LGBTIQA+ Writers* (2018), *Kindred: 12 Queer #LoveOzYA Stories (2019)* and *Growing up Queer in Australia* (2019).

Claire Candland is a writer and editor raising children in a land of salt and snow, red rock and the Rocky Mountains. Her hobbies include overthinking, writing absurd emails to strangers, and making music despite occasional bouts of disharmony. She is currently working on a full-length memoir. You can find her at ClaireCandland.com.

Stacy Cannatella lives outside of Boston with her wife and three daughters in a little house crammed full of children's drawings, furry animals, and love. Stacy has been a teacher, a carpenter, and a circus roustabout. She currently works as a writer and an editor.

Beth Cronin has been a social worker for over twenty years, working in both Australia and the United Kingdom. She has a deep interest in the human experience and the way socio-political contexts profoundly shape the narratives of our lives. Beth has a deep love of words, books, and poetry and is a passionate believer in the healing power of stories. She lives in northern New South Wales, Australia, with her loving wife Tanya and their spirited and outrageously loved son, Xander.

Patricia Curmi is a thirty-four-year old British parent of a toddler with a Mexican partner, both of whom identify (and are identified) as women. They both work part time in charities and higher education, and recently moved from the capital, London, to a small coastal town in the south of the United Kingdom. Since writing this piece, their second child was born, and they are having a t-shirt printed to answer The Question in advance. It reads: "Two kids, immaculate conception. No more questions without coffee."

Raechel Johns is an Australian marketing professor and parent. Raechel is passionate about service management and, in particular, supporting various vulnerable communities through her research and marketing work, including the LGBTIQ+ community, people with disabilities, foster children, and the ageing population, among others. She loves writing and enjoys writing both within her career and as a hobby. She also loves spending time with her family. Together, they especially love travelling, going to the beach, dining out, and watching movies.

Sonja Mackenzie is an associate professor in the Public Health Program at Santa Clara University. Her scholarship addresses disparities in health experienced by LGBTQ and racial/ethnic minority communities through research at the nexus of public health, sociology, and sexuality studies. She is the author of the book *Structural Intimacies: Sexual Stories in the Black AIDS Epidemic* (Rutgers University Press, 2013), numerous publications on HIV/AIDS and gender/sexuality, and has written for *The Huffington Post* and *The Advocate* as a queer parent and activist. Sonja was born and raised in Scotland and lives in the San Francisco Bay Area with her partner and two children.

Sherri Martin-Baron is the nonbiological and nongestational mother of three fabulous kids. She lives in upstate New York with her awesome wife and their brood. She teaches English to speakers of other languages at the college level. Grammar is her favourite subject. This is her first narrative piece as well as her first coediting project.

Nadja Miko-Schefzig, born in 1968, is Vinzent's comother. She studied philosophy, and today she is a management consultant in Vienna, Austria, in the field of diversity management, inclusive organization, communication, and leadership development. She used to work as a performance dramaturge and, at the beginning of her professional life, in a Styrofoam factory. During this time, she became involved as a queer activist and published on this topic, moderated philosophical salons, and organized queer parties and film events. Since 2004, she has been with Katharina, the biological mother of Vinzi, who was born in 2015.

Leah Oppenzato currently teaches seventh grade humanities at a progressive K-8 school in Hoboken, New Jersey. She also chairs the education committee at Kolot Chayeinu/Voices of Our Lives, a nondenominational Jewish congregation; writes lesson plans about the international right to freedom of assembly; and texts like mad to get out the vote for any U.S. Democratic candidate she can find. Other interests include the study of world religions and narrative writing. She lives in Brooklyn, NY, with her wife, son, daughter, dog, and gerbils.

Ryann Peyton is a queer activist, speaker, and lawyer. Ryann is a litigator and a seasoned consultant and advocate on diversity and equity in the legal field. Ryann focuses their law practice on civil litigation with an emphasis on LGBTQ family and civil rights. Ryann is also cofounder of RANGE Consulting, a social enterprise focused on training employers on strategies for LGBTQ workplace inclusivity. Ryann chairs the board of several queer nonprofit organizations in Colorado and was named a "2016 Thought Leader" by the Denver Business Journal. Ryann currently resides in Denver, Colorado, with their wife, Sara, and son, Archer.

Emily Regan Wills was born in the United States and raised in feminist and antiwar movements. She is currently a professor at the University of Ottawa, where she teaches American and comparative politics, researches transnationalism between North America and the Middle East, and codirects a project supporting community mobilization in displaced and marginalized communities in the Middle East and elsewhere. Outside of work, she sponsors LGBTQ refugees in

Canada and helps run her children's school council. She and her wife have two children, one born in Brooklyn, the other born in Ottawa.

Allie Robbins is the nonbiological mother of two children. She comoms with her wife, who is her son's biological mother. She is an associate professor of law at the City University of New York School of Law, where she has worked in a variety of teaching and administrative positions, all designed to educate and train social justice activist attorneys. Prior to working for CUNY Law School, she worked as an organizer and assistant counsel for the National Treasury Employees Union and as an organizer for United Students Against Sweatshops.

Louise Silver is an East Coast transplant who has made her home in the Bay Area, California, with her wife and two kids. As a career educator and instructional coach, she is passionate about attaining more equitable opportunities and outcomes for all children. Louise dedicates this, and any other writing she ever does, to her beloved and brilliant sister who passed away before she could catch her big break as a novelist.